וַיַּעֲשׂוּ כָל הַקָּהָל הַשָּׁבִים מִן הַשְּׁבִי סֻכּוֹת וַיֵּשְׁבוּ
בַסֻּכּוֹת כִּי לֹא עָשׂוּ מִימֵי יֵשׁוּעַ בִּן נוּן כֵּן בְּנֵי יִשְׂרָאֵל
עַד הַיּוֹם הַהוּא וַתְּהִי שִׂמְחָה גְדוֹלָה
עַד מְאֹד

Fecit ergo universa cœtum qui redierant de captivitate tabernacula et habitauerunt
in tabernaculis non enim fecerant a diebus Iosue filij num taliter filijs Israel
usq ad diem illum et suit lætisia magna nimis   מי פעל ועשה בן שבעים וששה

matzia Gußzyglich fecit 8bre 1813   Neemia Cap. 8. W. 17.

In the JEWISH TRADITION

A Year of Food and Festivities

Judith B. Fellner

SMITHMARK

The publisher would like to thank A.C. Fellner for permission to reproduce the following text:
Page 14, "The Hebrew Calendar"; page 19, "The Shofar: Prayer Without Words"; page 28, "The Kol Nidrei Prayer";
page 32, "The Story of Jonah"; page 57, "Lysias, the Greek General"; page 70, "Bigthan and Teresh are Dead";
page 73, "Amalek: the Eternal Enemy"; page 85, "Hametz: the Ultimate Contaminant";
page 87, "The Haggadah: A Book for All Generations"; page 90, "Elijah: Prophet and Symbol";
page 102, "The Omer"; page 104, "What is Torah"; and page 106, "The Scrolls of Ruth and Esther."

A FRIEDMAN GROUP BOOK

This edition published in 1995 by SMITHMARK Publishers, Inc.
16 East 32nd Street, New York NY 10016

SMITHMARK Books are available for bulk purchase for sales promotion and premium use. For details write or call the
manager of special sales, SMITHMARK Publishers Inc., 16 East 32nd Street, New York NY 10016; (212) 532-6600

ISBN 0-8317-5268-8

IN THE JEWISH TRADITION
A Year of Food and Festivities
was prepared and produced by
Michael Friedman Publishing Group, Inc.
15 West 26th Street
New York, NY 10010

Fellner, Judith B.
    In the Jewish tradition : a year of foods and festivities / Judith
B. Fellner.
        p.   cm.
    Includes index.
    ISBN 0-8317-5268-8 (hardcover)
    1. Fasts and feasts--Judaism. 2. Holiday cookery. 3. Cookery,
Jewish. I. Title
BM690.F418 1995
296.4'3--dc20   95-20800
                                                    CIP

Editor: Sharon Kalman
Art Director: Jeff Batzli
Designer: Elan Studio
Music typography: Tom Garber
Photography Director: Christopher C. Bain
Photography Editor: Wendy Missan
Production Manager: Jeanne E. Kaufman

Color separations by Bright Arts (Singapore) Pte. Ltd.
Printed in Hong Kong and bound in China by Midas Printing Limited

10 9 8 7 6 5 4 3 2 1

Table of CONTENTS

To Azriel,

whose support and love made this book possible.

PREFACE

A book is never all you dream it could be; your vision is always larger than reality. At some point, you realize that no matter what the vision and revisions, it can always be better; no matter how careful the research, there are always mistakes. And so the time comes to let go, and allow the book its own existence.

The road to creating this book was not a smooth one. Along the way I had major back surgery, which seriously impaired progress on the book and hampered my mobility for months. But even that experience was valuable, for during my extended convalescence, I delved more deeply within myself and came to create a far different book from the one I had begun. In an odd way, I owe a debt to that experience, which forced me to reach beyond myself and my own discomfort, and give myself over completely to the subject matter.

I wish to express appreciation to several individuals who generously gave of themselves and their time. My sister Laurie patiently put menus and recipes into a laptop computer and gave me invaluable suggestions for the book. My brother, Jonathan, was an efficient fact-checker. My sister Linda was always a dependable source of succor and support.

I especially thank Dr. Mayer Rabinowitz, librarian of the Jewish Theological Seminary, and Dr. Neil Gillman, Associate Professor of Philosophy at the Jewish Theological Seminary, who, on short notice, read the manuscript and made some pertinent comments, many of which I have incorporated. Dr. Shaye J. D. Cohen, Ungerleider Professor of Judaic Studies at Brown University, and Dr. Anne Lapidus Lerner, Vice-Chancellor of the Jewish Theological Seminary, both extended me valuable assistance for which I am most grateful. Cantor Avima Darnoff and Ruthie Cohen helped with the music. A very special thanks to Velvel Pasternak of TARA Publications for not only his musical expertise, but his graciousness.

For the resource section at the back of the book, I gratefully acknowledge assistance from Joseph B. Sandler, Director of the United Synagogue Book Service; Carolyn Starman Hessel of the Jewish Book Council; Renee Savitz of Precious Heirlooms; Ilene Greenbaum, librarian of Temple Beth Shalom; and Marilyn Breitman, Judaic librarian.

The office staff of Temple Beth Shalom, Livingston, New Jersey, especially Evelyn Frank, extended technical assistance for which I am most appreciative.

I wish to express special gratitude to Sharyn Rosart, editorial director of Michael Friedman Publishing Group, for her many kindnesses to me, her sensitivity, and her unwavering enthusiasm for the project and faith in me. I also wish to thank Sharon Kalman for editing the manuscript and her cooperation in incorporating my many changes. Wendy Missan, the photography editor, went out of her way to work with me to ensure the photographs reflected the spirit of the book and I am indebted to her. Thanks to Lori Thorn, the designer, Loretta Mowat, production editor, Tom Garber, who did a wonderful job of music typography, and all the production people at Michael Friedman Publishing Group whose expertise lent beauty to the final product.

My daughter Michelle edited several chapters before submission, tested several of the recipes, and helped refine the menus, and my daughter Tamar gave me constructive feedback and cheerfully retyped several chapters of the book with her usual efficiency after my computer crashed. To both of them a very special thank you.

My mother, Mary Marks, provided the excellent and creative holiday meals of my youth, which have influenced my own cooking as well as the notebooks for this book.

I wish above all to thank my husband, Azriel, who had the forbearance to put up with a roomful of books, who generously gave many hours to the writing of many of the creative and informational sidebars, and who directed me to sources when I needed them. The homes we both came from and the one we built together, the memories of holidays warmly celebrated with our parents, and later, our children, and our extended families provided the inspiration for this book.

ag means holiday in Hebrew; in Arabic, *Hajj* refers to the Islamic sacred journey or pilgrimage to Mecca during Ramadan. This book is about holidays and sacred journeys—not one, but many. This book has taken me on sacred journeys to different periods in Jewish history where I could explore the fascinating twists and turns in the road of the development of the Jewish holidays.

The road is often not a clear and straight path, but one that is obscured by historical clouds that make its course hard to trace with any certainty. There is much guesswork, because there is much that is not known about the evolution of certain Jewish holidays, like Rosh Hashanah and, to some degree, Passover; often, the best that scholars can do is to propose theories. A holiday such as Hanukkah may have left clearer historical imprints, but still requires study, analysis, and evaluation of sources to piece together the history and story with any accuracy.

One comes away with a remarkable appreciation of Judaism after studying the evolution, customs, and traditions of the Jewish holidays. One can see evidence of the genius of both rabbinic Judaism and the Jewish people, who exert a mutually beneficial and even synergistic influence upon each other.

Jewish agricultural festivals become historical ones as well. Shavuot, which in the Bible is the wheat harvest holiday, becomes, in the hands of the Rabbis, the time of the giving of the Torah. It thereby joins the other pilgrimage festivals of Passover and Sukkot to commemorate the Exodus as both a historical event and a process—the event of leaving Egypt, and the process of the children of Israel becoming a people. The historical emphasis is what enabled the holidays not only to survive, but to thrive.

But the Jewish holidays did not develop in a vacuum. The cultures under which the Jews lived exerted an influence, whether Canaanitic, Babylonian, Roman, Greek, Spanish, German, or, for many of us, American. What made the Jewish holidays unique is that the Jewish people, while often influenced by local customs and festivals, cast a specifically Jewish form on each holiday. Therefore, Jewish holidays are remarkably devoid of pagan, mythological, or magical influences.

The peculiarly Jewish character of the holidays is what transforms a Roman banquet into a seder, makes Rosh Hashanah a time for introspection, and makes Purim a time for giving treats to friends and gifts to the poor.

Opposite: A Sukkot meal. (See page 50.) Above: A nineteenth-century woodcut from Poland with the words "You shall dwell in booths seven days" (Lev. 23:42).

I have endeavored in this book to show what we know of the development of the Jewish holidays and to describe how the holidays are currently celebrated, incorporating the changes that have come about in Conservative and Reform Judaism, which were influenced by the feminist revolution that began in the 1970s. Women in many congregations are now serving as cantors and rabbis, and Jewish women are taking on many of the previously all-male practices, such as donning *tallilot* (prayer shawls) and reading from the Torah.

In each chapter, there is a section of customs and traditions to give the reader quick and easy access to the most common practices associated with each holiday and some less common ones as well. Wherever possible, I have tried to distinguish between pure custom—such as sending out greeting cards for Rosh Hashanah—and law—such as abstaining from food on Yom Kippur.

One of my goals in writing this book was to go beyond the critical history and development, customs and traditions, delicious foods, and good times. I wanted to bare the soul and uncover the essence of each holiday. What is the meaning behind the Days of Awe? What does a sukkah really signify? How is Passover to be understood? What lessons do we derive from Hanukkah? What is Shavuot really about?

I have also tried to make a smooth transition between the holidays by linking each holiday with the previous one, so that they become interconnected and are not seen as isolated and without context. For example, I was able to link Hanukkah to Sukkot because originally, Hanukkah was celebrated as a second Sukkot and therefore has retained many of Sukkot's characteristics. I've linked Purim to Hanukkah (both minor holidays, post-

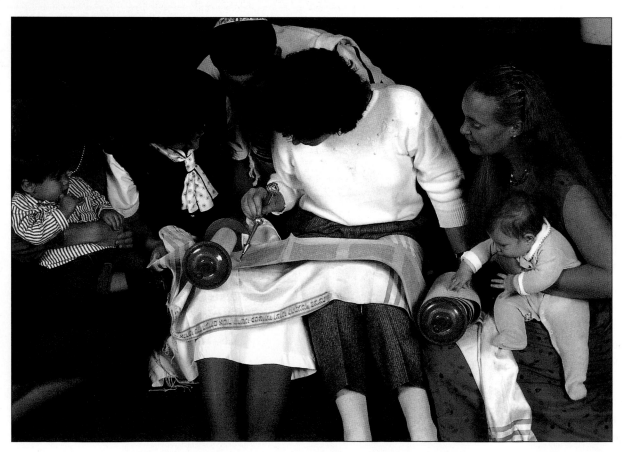

A group of Jewish women gather for Torah reading on Simhat Torah.

א י ע ד — ד ל א י ע ד

A nineteenth-century folk art painting of a Hasidic rabbi (right) drinking on Purim with a Sephardic rabbi (left).

biblically ordained), one decreed by the Maccabees, the other by Mordecai and Esther. Some of the links are natural ones, such as the relationship of Shavuot to Passover, or Yom Kippur to Rosh Hashanah.

At the end of each chapter is a special section entitled *Hiddur Mitzvah*, which I have liberally translated as "enhancing the holiday." The concept of *hiddur mitzvah* is based upon the biblical verse "This is my Lord and I will glorify Him" (Exod. 15:2). In the Talmud, the Rabbis spell out how to adorn God and concluded that it should be done by fulfilling the commandments in the most exemplary manner possible. Hence, they taught, for example, that a sukkah should be very attractive—one should acquire the finest specimens of the lulav and etrog—and a shofar should be exceptionally beautiful. The concept is to go beyond the legal requirements into the realm of aesthetics—to do more than is strictly required by law as a way of glorifying God. The purpose of the *Hiddur Mitzvah* section is to show how the concept of beautifying the ritual and enhancing religious practice can be applied creatively to each holiday to bring extra warmth, joy, and beauty into the home.

The informational sidebars, together with stories, poetry, and songs, are intended to expand upon the text. Included are ancient as well as modern literary sources and musical material.

Following each chapter are recipes and menus. This part of the book is geared toward the kosher cook in the kosher kitchen. All recipes are in accordance with the laws of kashrut.

The festival table should be beautifully set with fine china, silver, and crystal. Fresh flowers are always a wonderful touch. Two *hallot* (under a beautiful cover) and wine should be placed on the festival table when required. Candlelighting should be done before *yom tov*, and the appropriate kiddush to the holiday recited. *Birkat Hamazon*, Grace after Meals, follows the meal.

While I do not purport to be a professional cook, my expertise in the kitchen derives from about twenty-five years of experimenting and entertaining for the Jewish holidays. I have always loved to cook, and the recipes, many of which were generously supplied by friends and family members, are a blend of the traditional and the more innovative. Reflecting modern cooking trends, I have included many recipes for the health-conscious, featuring whole grains, fruits, vegetables, and salads. For those who like to splurge occasionally, especially on the holidays, calorie caution is thrown to the wind in the rich desserts I have included. Feel free to experiment. New flavors and taste sensations can often be created by substituting one ingredient for another—one herb for another, one kind of nut for another—and the recipe will not suffer in the least.

Many of the recipes were compiled with vegetarians in mind. The Shavuot section includes two separate menus, to give more choices for vegetarians and to be able to include recipes for both cheesecake and cheese blintzes.

In the back of the book is music for the songs and a resource guide for the purchase of books and of Judaica, audio-visual, and multi-media materials.

I'd like to think of this book as an adventure—an adventure in exploring the Jewish heritage and an adventure in eating. This book is geared to those who do not know much about the Jewish holidays, but want to know more, as well as those who are well-informed, but want a more sophisticated approach. I hope this book serves as an important and memorable stop on your journey into the world of Jewish festivities and foods.

Judith B. Fellner
Livingston, New Jersey
November 1994, Kislev 5755

CHAPTER ONE

ROSH HASHANAH

osh Hashanah heads the year of Jewish festivities, foods, and traditions. Jews around the world celebrate their New Year, known as Rosh Hashanah, in September or October, depending upon when it falls in the lunisolar Hebrew calendar (see page 14). Other names for the Jewish New Year are *Yom Hazikaron* (Day of Remembrance) and *Yom Hadin* (Judgment Day).

The name "Rosh Hashanah," meaning "head of the year," is a rabbinic designation for the holiday. In the Hebrew Bible, there is no mention of Rosh Hashanah as such. It was observed as a holiday, but how it was celebrated and the form it took is still unknown. The festival is simply referred to either as "a sacred occasion commemorated with loud blasts" (Lev. 23:24) or as "the day of the blowing of the horn" (*Yom Teruah*), "And in the seventh month, on the first day of the month, you shall observe a special occasion; you shall not work at your occupations: you shall observe it as a day of the blowing of the horn" (Num. 29:1).

THE SEVENTH MONTH

How the first day of the seventh month (the month of Tishri) became the Jewish New Year and evolved into such a significant holiday still mystifies scholars and does not seem to have a clear answer. It is, after all, Passover that falls on the first month of the biblical calendar in spring (Nisan), and all Jewish holidays are determined in relation to Passover, the first of the pilgrimage festivals. It has been suggested that the bibli-

cal holiday of the "blowing of the horn" on the first day of the seventh month might have become a glorified new moon and developed from there. All new moons were occasions for celebration, but the new moon closest to the autumn harvest, when certain ancient Semitic peoples like the Canaanites thought the year began (as the old agricultural year ended), might have become more prominent than the others.

The new moon of the seventh month also may have become especially important because the number seven in the Hebrew Bible is a special number. It is associated with holiness and completion. The most sacred day of the week, Shabbat, is on the seventh day of the week. The important Sabbatical year when the land lies fallow and debts are forgiven occurs every seventh year. The Jubilee (the freeing of slaves and the remission of land to its original owners)

Opposite: Blowing the shofar.
Above: This New Year's card depicts the sounding of the shofar.

occurs on the fiftieth year after seven cycles of seven years have been completed. Seven weeks are counted from Passover until Shavuot. There are seven branches on the menorah in the Tabernacle, and seven species of produce grown in the land of Israel are singled out in the Bible.

Therefore, "the day of the blowing of the horn," falling as it does on the new moon of the seventh month near the autumn harvest festival (beginning a new season of rainfall and fertility), might have helped it develop into a festival of real importance.

It is significant that the religious leader Ezra, who had returned from Babylonian exile, chose the first day of the seventh month to read sections of the Torah to the assembled people by the water gate in Jerusalem. Although they wept in response, realizing their neglect of Jewish law and life, they were urged to joyfully celebrate that day because it was holy. Their contrite response and subsequent commitment to a course of spiritual renewal under God's authority may have further contributed to Rosh Hashanah's development.

UNIVERSALITY OF ROSH HASHANAH

Whatever its obscure origins and development, by Tannaitic times (first and second centuries C.E.), Rosh Hashanah had evolved and begun to resemble the holiday we now celebrate. Unlike other Jewish holidays, Rosh Hashanah is one of the few Jewish festivals that has neither an agricultural nor a historical basis. In fact, the Jewish New Year is not at all limited to the Jewish experience because it celebrates the birthday of the world. According to Jewish tradition, all peoples and nations are judged on Rosh Hashanah, not just Jews. Each person's fate is determined during the *Yamim Noraim*, the Days of Awe (Rosh Hashanah and the intervening days through Yom Kippur).

According to rabbinic imagination, during the Days of Awe three books are open before God: one for the wholly

THE HEBREW CALENDAR

The Hebrew months of the Jewish calendar are determined by the moon, and the Jewish year by the sun. Hence, the Jewish calendar is known as lunisolar. Since the solar year is approximately 365 days long and the length of a lunar month can either be twenty-nine or thirty days in length, the disparity between the year as calculated by the sun and the year as calculated by the moon comes to a loss of approximately eleven days each year. Over a period of years, a festival that should occur in the spring, like Passover, would "wander" through the calendar.

As a result, rabbinic authorities who were experts in both astronomy and mathematical calculations added an additional month within predictable yearly cycles so that the holidays would always fall within the proper and appropriate season. So skillful were some of the Rabbis in dealing with the calendar that they were also able to make sure that certain festivals would never fall on certain days, making it difficult if not impossible for the Jewish people to observe the festival. For example, the Rabbis shaped the calendar so that Yom Kippur, the Day of Atonement, could never fall directly before or after the Sabbath.

The festivals (Passover, Shavuot, Sukkot, Rosh Hashanah, and Yom Kippur) were all fixed on certain dates within the lunar month by the Torah. In ancient times, before the calendar was finally fixed through astronomical calculations, each new month was announced through the sighting of the new moon, and that sighting was ratified by a court in Jerusalem that was expert in such matters. Those who lived within a certain distance of Jerusalem would receive the ratification of that sighting in ample time to make preparations for the festival. Those living far away, however, where news could not travel in a timely fashion, or where information might be unreliable, needed to establish two festival days instead of one to be sure that they observed the correct day of the holiday. These two-day festivals became a sacred

part of the calendar for those who lived in the Diaspora (outside the land of Israel). And even after the Rabbis could easily predict when the new month would begin, the second-day celebration of the holidays in the Diaspora nevertheless continued and does so to the present day. Only the Reform movement has formally abolished the second day of the festival.

Today in Israel, Jews celebrate the festivals for one day, with the exception of Rosh Hashanah, where two days are observed. Furthermore, the actual day begins at sundown. Thus, in the Hebrew calendar, a full day runs from sundown to sundown.

Some of the holidays begin and end with festival days when no work is permitted. The days in between are called *Hol Hamoed*, or "half holidays," when work is permitted, but in a restricted manner.

The Hebrew month of Nisan is considered the first month of the year and takes its name from the Babylonian *Nissanu*, which means "to start." The reigns of biblical kings were numbered from the month of Nisan, and, according to Rabbi Joshua, the world was created during this month. Other rabbinic authorities, however, started the year with Tishri, the month during which Rosh Hashanah, the New Year, is celebrated, and so it has remained to this day.

For all intents and purposes, however, the New Year—which begins in Tishri and inaugurates the solemn festivals of Rosh Hashanah followed by Yom Kippur—is a kind of personal inventory and accounting of life, an inward spiritual period in the calendar. Six months later, Nisan might also be considered a new beginning, the holiday of national renewal accompanied by the spring season and the rebirth of nature.

Thus, with adroit calculations, the Rabbis balanced the solar year against the lunar month and fashioned a calendar that fixes the holidays in their appropriate seasons, thereby preserving three thousand years of festivals and festivities.

righteous, one for the wholly wicked, and one for the average person. The wholly righteous are immediately inscribed and sealed in the book of life; the wholly evil, in the book of death; and those in between—the vast majority—are held in suspension until Yom Kippur.

It is during this time that one seeks forgiveness of God and especially of one's fellow human being. While Yom Kippur allows us to atone for sins against God, people must seek forgiveness directly from the persons they wrong in order to achieve full atonement. It is likewise incumbent upon those who have been wronged during the year to forgive with a full heart those who request it. According to the *Shulhan Arukh* (a sixteenth-century authoritative code of Jewish law) the person who is generous and forgiving will in turn have his or her own sins forgiven. The Days of Awe, or High Holy Days, are therefore a time for genuine conciliation and reconciliation.

An ornamental page with rules for Rosh Hashanah from the Rothschild Mahzor, Florence, Italy, 1492. The Mahzor is the prayerbook used on the High Holy Days.

Master of the Universe! I herewith forgive anyone who may have irritated, angered, or injured me, whether acting against my person, my possessions, or my reputation. Let no human being be punished on my account, whether the wrong done me was accidental or malicious, unwitting or purposeful, by word or by deed. May it be Your will, O Lord my God and God of my fathers, that I not repeat the wrongs I have committed, and that I sin no more. May I never again anger You by doing that which is evil in Your sight. I pray that You will wipe away my sins, not through sickness and suffering but with great mercy. May the words of my mouth and the meditation of my heart be acceptable before You, O Lord, my Rock and my Redeemer.

THE SOUL IS YOURS

The soul is Yours, the body is Your work;
O Lord, have compassion upon Your labor.
The soul is Yours, the body is Your work;
O Lord, save us for Your name's sake.

We come before You in Your name;
For Your glorious name, help us,
You are called gracious and merciful;
Forgive, then, our sin, though it is great.

> Forgive us, our Father!
> With great folly have we gone astray.
> Pardon us, our King!
> Our sins have overwhelmed us.

Selihot Prayer. Reprinted from *Selihot*, edited by Rabbi Gershon Hadas. © 1964 by the Rabbinical Assembly. Reprinted by permission of the Rabbinical Assembly.

SPIRITUAL PREPARATION FOR THE HIGH HOLY DAYS

As for any important event, preparation is critical; this is especially true for the High Holy Days. The High Holy Day season begins one month before Rosh Hashanah in the beginning of the month of Elul when the *shofar*, or ram's horn, is customarily blown each day after morning services and Sephardic Jews begin to recite penitential prayers known as *Selihot*. On the Saturday evening before Rosh Hashanah, Ashkenazic Jews gather in the stillness of night around midnight—technically Sunday—to recite some of the most moving of the *Selihot* prayers, in which the major musical motifs for the High Holy Days are heard the first time. This becomes the spiritual overture to the High Holy Day period, which reaches a crescendo on Yom Kippur.

TIME TO TAKE STOCK

Rosh Hashanah is celebrated for two days by Conservative and Orthodox Jews and in Israel, for it is referred to in the Talmud (the encyclopedic compilation of rabbinic writings, discussions, and teachings, which include the Mishnah and Gemara, circa 200–550 C.E. See also page 104.) as *Yoma Arikhta*—a prolonged day. Most Reform Jews, however, observe only one day of Rosh Hashanah.

Rosh Hashanah is the time to put one's spiritual house in order, much as Passover is the time to clean out one's physical surroundings. What is distinctive about the Jewish New Year is that unlike other (secular) New Year celebrations, it is a time of

In this introspective photo, a grandfather teaches his grandson in Biala, Poland, as the grandmother looks on.

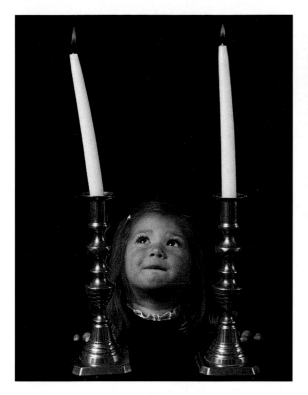

repentance, reflection, and renewal, not revelry and rowdiness. It is time for taking stock and for self-evaluation. It is a time to look back but also to look forward.

During the High Holy Day period, there is an acute awareness of the finiteness and precariousness of life, of the fleetingness of time, and consequently of the importance of using time wisely. For the believing Jew, it means that life has purpose and one's actions matter. It means taking responsibility, rectifying past errors, assuming control, and changing course if necessary. It is the time to reflect on the meaning of success and failure and to concentrate on life's meaning and purpose and one's place in the universe. As a result, Rosh Hashanah, unlike other Jewish festivals, is not a home celebration as much as a synagogue holy day given to public prayer and private introspection.

ROSH HASHANAH LITURGY

The prayerbook used on the High Holy Days is called the *Mahzor*. The prayers on Rosh Hashanah reflect the themes of repentance (*teshuvah*); of God as king, judge, recorder of human history, and architect of human destiny; of the evanescence of life; and of human vulnerability and fragility. Among the distinctive prayers for Rosh Hashanah are *piyyutim*, medieval liturgical poems often written in acrostic form.

The best-known prayer for Rosh Hashanah is the *Unetaneh Tokef*, attributed to Rabbi Amnon, a tenth-century martyr, although his authorship and even his existence have been challenged. The prayer vividly and poignantly describes how each human being passes before God for review, and how a person's fate

SHAAREI TESHUVA

Birth is a beginning
And death a destination.
And life is a journey:
From childhood to maturity
And youth to age;
From innocence to awareness
And ignorance to knowing;
From foolishness to discretion
    And then, perhaps, to wisdom;
From weakness to strength
Or strength to weakness—
    And, often, back again;
From health to sickness
    And back, we pray, to health again;
From offense to forgiveness,
From loneliness to love,
From joy to gratitude,
From pain to compassion,
And grief to understanding—
    From fear to faith;
From defeat to defeat to defeat—
Until, looking backward or ahead,
We see that victory lies
Not at some high place along the way,
But in having made the journey, stage by stage,
    A sacred pilgrimage.
Birth is a beginning....

is determined on Rosh Hashanah and sealed on Yom Kippur. *"This day all who walk the earth pass You as a flock of sheep. And like a shepherd who gathers his flock bringing them under his staff, You bring everything before You for review. You determine the life and decree the destiny of every creature."* The *Unetaneh Tokef* prayer beautifully captures both the solemnity and fearsomeness of the season with unforgettable imagery, but climaxes on the heartening note that *"repentance, prayer, and righteous acts can avert the harshness of the decree."*

The richest service on Rosh Hashanah day is the *Musaf*, or additional service. Just before the *Musaf*, the cantor chants a prayer called *Hineni*, which expresses the cantor's humility before God, for it is important to both the cantor and the congregation to pray with good intent.

One of the unique features of the *Musaf* service is a three-part liturgical addition that reflects the themes of Rosh Hashanah. Each part begins with an introduction followed by ten scriptural verses. The first part, known as *Malkhuyot*, emphasizes the sovereignty of God: God as ruler, judge, and king over all. The second part, *Zikhronot*, speaks of God's comprehensive and infallible memory. It is an appeal to His compassion as the judge of human beings and nations, and the architect of human history and destiny. The third part, *Shofarot*, refers to God's revelation at Sinai amid sounds of the shofar, and to a future redemption that the shofar proclaims. The sounding of the shofar closes each of these sections.

THE SHOFAR

The ritual most closely associated with Rosh Hashanah is the sounding of the shofar. A shofar is preferably made from a ram's horn, but the horn of any kosher animal is acceptable. A horn from a cow or an ox is never used, because that would have negative undertones—a reminder of the sin of the golden calf, the calf constructed by Moses' brother, Aaron, and worshipped by the Israelites during Moses' long absence on Mount Sinai. The ram's horn, on the other hand, is a reminder of the "binding of Isaac," the *akedah*, when Abraham proved his devotion to God through his willingness to sacrifice his beloved son Isaac; in the end, through Divine intervention, he sacrificed a ram instead. It is the Torah reading for the second day of Rosh Hashanah.

Distinctive sounds of the shofar include the *tekiah*, a long blast; the *shevarim*, three short blasts; and the *teruah*, nine staccato blasts. The shofar is sounded in a specific order and is blown in many synagogues a hundred times in the course of the Rosh Hashanah service. It is never sounded on the Sabbath because the Rabbis feared a violation of the Shabbat through carrying, for example, which was prohibited on Shabbat.

According to Maimonides, the great medieval Jewish philosopher and commentator, the shofar is an awakening call. Its purpose is to rouse Jews from their slumber, from complacency and self-satisfaction. It is a call to both reflection and action, thought and deed.

REPENTANCE AND CHANGE

The call to reflection and action is particularly heeded during the *Aseret Yemei Teshuvah*, the ten days of repentance between Rosh Hashanah and Yom Kippur. During this time, thoughts turn inward to self-examination, and deeds of lovingkindness are increased with the approach of Yom Kippur.

The Sabbath before Yom Kippur is known as Shabbat Shuvah, the Sabbath of Return, based on the prophetic reading from the Book of Hosea beginning "Return O Israel" (Hosea 14:2).

Teshuvah, the Hebrew word for repentance, can also mean "return." It is the key word of the High Holy Day period, for it is the means provided to atone for one's sins and to emerge reborn. It is an expression of hope, encouragement, and possibility. The Rabbis included repentance as one of the seven things that preceded the creation of the world, thereby emphasizing its importance. Teshuvah is a return to God and to a state of inner wholeness. According to the Rabbis, it is never too late to repent—a person can even repent on his deathbed. Rabbi Simeon Bar Yohai, a rabbi who lived during the Roman period, once said that even if a person is completely wicked all his life, but repents at the end of his life, he is not to be reproached for his wickedness. The Rabbis thought that a penitent sinner was more praiseworthy than a totally righteous person or saintly individual.

This ability to change one's fate is the thread that runs through the High Holy Days. Although there is an awareness of death and human limitations, Rosh Hashanah emphasizes life and its possibilities. There are new pages of life to be written and fresh chapters to be lived, important heights to climb, and worthy goals to reach.

Rosh Hashanah therefore is a sober, but not somber, holiday. Rosh Hashanah emphasizes life more than death; hope not despair. Rosh Hashanah expresses the belief in human potential for change and growth. Nothing is static; people are not stuck. Humanity itself is ultimately redeemable through change of heart and action. This is one of Rosh Hashanah's most powerful messages.

TRADITIONS AND CUSTOMS ASSOCIATED WITH ROSH HASHANAH

- Blowing the Shofar after morning services during the month of Elul, preceding Rosh Hashanah until the day before Rosh Hashanah, except on the Sabbath.
- Reciting Psalm 27 from the beginning of Elul until *Hoshana Rabbah*.
- Visiting the graves of one's relatives and friends during the month of Elul.

- Greeting people with the words *Shanah tovah umetukah* (Have a good and sweet year!), or *L'shanah tovah tikateivu* (May you be written into the Book of Life!). Between Rosh Hashanah and Yom Kippur it is customary to greet people with *L'shanah tovah tikateivu vetehateimu* (May you be inscribed and sealed in the Book of Life), and after Rosh Hashanah through Hoshana Rabbah, *G'mar hatimah tovah* (May you end up with a good sealing [in the Book of Life]).
- Sending New Year's cards to friends and relatives is a popular American Jewish custom that may have originated in Germany.
- Dipping pieces of apple and hallah (egg bread) in honey instead of salt, and reciting the following prayer at the beginning of the festive meal: "*Yehi ratzon mil'fanekha Adonai Eloheinu V'Elohei avoteinu she'tehadesh aleinu shanah tovah*

PRAYER WITHOUT WORDS: THE SHOFAR

When the time comes for the shofar to be sounded in the synagogue, a hush comes over the congregation and tension begins to mount. The sound of the shofar is raw and austere, and only an accomplished shofar blower is able to create the sounds required. The requirement to hear the sounds of the shofar falls only upon men, but this part of the service is so popular that everyone comes to synagogue on this day to hear it.

The shofar is among the oldest instruments in the world. It was used to call people to war, to gather the community for announcements, to serve as musical accompaniment for the coronation of a king, and to create an atmosphere of awe and fear. The shofar was sounded at Mount Sinai when the Ten Commandments were about to be given, and as a proclamation of freedom during the Jubilee year (see page 13) for all indentured servants. It was also used together with other instruments, such as the trumpet, in Temple times.

The shofar is made of one of five species of animal: sheep, goat, mountain goat, antelope, or gazelle. The ram or the wild goat's horn is preferable because they are both curved, and of these two, the ram's horn is the one used most often because it is a reminder of the ram that was substituted by Abraham for Isaac during the *akedah* (see page 18). The shofar must be plain, without defect: a natural instrument in a natural state.

In the Torah (Num. 29:1), Rosh Hashanah is designated as *Yom Teruah*, "a day of blowing." By the rabbinic period, exactly what constitutes the various sounds which were to be made on the shofar became a matter for discussion. Today, the sounds are a *tekiah*, a long blast, followed by three broken sounds—*shevarim*—followed by nine staccato bursts—*teruah*—and then another long sound—*tekiah*. Various patterns of these sounds were composed by the Rabbis so that the listeners would be able to fulfill the commandment of hearing the sounds of the shofar. After Temple times, however, the shofar was not sounded when Rosh Hashanah fell on the Sabbath, for fear that the instrument might be carried from one's domicile to the synagogue, and carrying on the Sabbath is forbidden.

Rabbis and interpreters suggest many reasons for the hearing of the shofar on the first two days of Rosh Hashanah. As an alarm clock awakens the sleeper, so the shofar awakens the spiritually dormant soul. Just as the shofar was once a call to war, so it is now a call to arms against what is evil and torpid within the human being. And just as the shofar once called a community together to free each individual, so it is now a call for each community to repair broken relationships among ethnic groups, to remember that all humanity is one, and that each person is a unique creation worthy of respect. In a larger sense, however, the shofar is like a cry, an inarticulate but deeply felt response to a year now gone and beyond reclamation. The beginning of a New Year is now upon us demanding attention, because time has become all the more precious.

Like the long sound of *tekiah*, where life appears unbroken, the listener also acknowledges that the *shevarim*, the broken sounds, are reflective of one's broken promises, and the *teruah*, the nine staccato bursts, are the spiritual ruptures within the heart.

The final sounding of the shofar is always the *tekiah gedolah*, the long blast. Rosh Hashanah delivers the hope of another year in which accomplishment, inner growth, and another chance await everyone.

Ushering in the New Year at the Western Wall in Jerusalem.

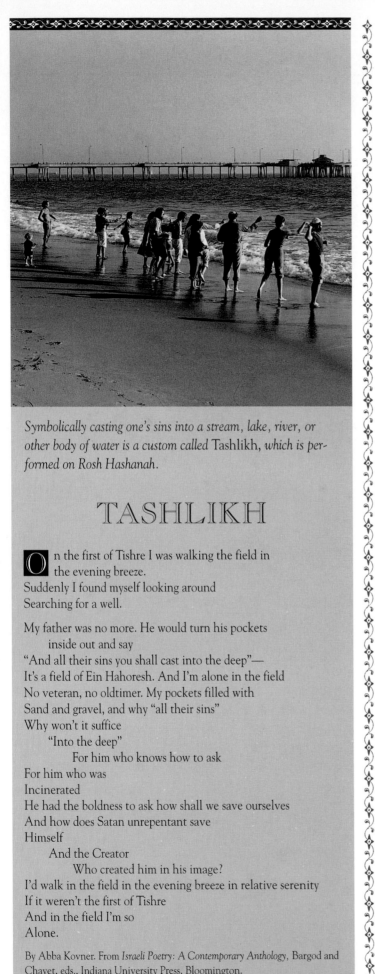

Symbolically casting one's sins into a stream, lake, river, or other body of water is a custom called Tashlikh, *which is performed on Rosh Hashanah.*

TASHLIKH

On the first of Tishre I was walking the field in the evening breeze.
Suddenly I found myself looking around
Searching for a well.

My father was no more. He would turn his pockets
        inside out and say
"And all their sins you shall cast into the deep"—
It's a field of Ein Hahoresh. And I'm alone in the field
No veteran, no oldtimer. My pockets filled with
Sand and gravel, and why "all their sins"
Why won't it suffice
        "Into the deep"
                For him who knows how to ask
For him who was
Incinerated
He had the boldness to ask how shall we save ourselves
And how does Satan unrepentant save
Himself
        And the Creator
                Who created him in his image?
I'd walk in the field in the evening breeze in relative serenity
If it weren't the first of Tishre
And in the field I'm so
Alone.

By Abba Kovner. From *Israeli Poetry: A Contemporary Anthology*, Bargod and Chayet, eds., Indiana University Press, Bloomington.

umetukah" (May it be Your will, O Lord our God and God of our fathers, that You renew for us a good and sweet year).

- One of the most important Jewish blessings is the *shehehe'yanu*, which is recited on every new occasion or event in the cycle of the year, including the first nights of holidays. Since Rosh Hashanah is the beginning of the New Year, the *shehehe'yanu* blessing is recited at candlelighting time, and at kiddush over wine. The blessing is: *Barukh atah Adonai Eloheinu melekh ha'olam shehehe'yanu v'kiymanu v'higiyanu laz'man hazeh.* (Blessed are You O Lord Our God king of the universe who has kept us in life, sustained us, and enabled us to reach this moment).

- On the second night of Rosh Hashanah, an exotic fruit not tasted in a season, such as a pomegranate, persimmon, papaya, mango, kiwi, or Asian pear is placed on the table. It is kept in mind when reciting the *shehehe'yanu* at candlelighting or at kiddush. After kiddush the fruit is dipped into honey and eaten.

- Serving two round sweet hallot (often made with raisins) symbolizing the roundness and fullness of life. Some think the round hallah resembles a crown and see it as a symbol of the kingship of God.

- Wearing new clothes to experience a sense of newness and to feel special on the New Year.

- *Tashlikh*: On the afternoon of the first day of Rosh Hashanah (the second day if the first day is on Shabbat), some Jews go to a body of water, shake out their pockets, drop crumbs into the water, and recite prayers about casting off sins and repentance, excerpted from the prophet Micah and other texts. "You will again have compassion upon us subduing our sins, casting all our sins into the depths of the sea" (Mic. 7:19).

Hiddur Mitzvah (Enhancing the Holiday)

Use non-drip creamed honey or a flavored honey (like cinnamon honey) for a creative touch. There are many beautiful glass, ceramic, or metal honey containers available to enhance the Rosh Hashanah table. Try various seasonal apples (Winesap, Gala, Red Delicious, Jonathan, Stayman, Cortland, and McIntosh) for dipping into honey.

An attractive honey jar graces the Rosh Hashanah table. Apples and hallah are customarily dipped into honey for a sweet New Year.

A Rosh Hashanah table set with a round hallah, which symbolizes the roundness and fullness of life. The hallah often contains raisins.

ROSH HASHANAH MENU

The menu for Rosh Hashanah is festive and elaborate, as befits a feast.
There is no salt on the table and the emphasis is on sweet dishes.
Among the traditional dishes are tzimmes and honey cake.

Round Holiday Hallah
Sweet and Sour Meatballs
Autumn Vegetable Soup
Mixed Green Salad with Raspberry Vinaigrette Dressing
Glazed Turkey Breast
Savory Couscous
Cranberry Applesauce
Carrot Tzimmes
Deluxe Honey Cake
or
Poached Pears in Wine Sauce
Sugar and Spice Cookies
Bowl of Green, Red, and Purple Grapes

Round Holiday Hallah

This rich and delicious hallah recipe was given to me by Faye Wasser of Clifton, New Jersey. I have made very minor changes.

- 5 to 6 cups flour
- ¼ cup honey or 6 tablespoons sugar
- 1½ teaspoons salt
- 1 package dry yeast
- ½ cup pareve margarine, softened
- 1 cup *hot* tap water
- 4 eggs (at room temperature), one egg separated
- ½ cup raisins (optional)
- 1 teaspoon cold water

In a large bowl, mix 1¼ cups of flour, the honey or sugar, salt, and undissolved yeast. Add margarine and hot tap water and beat 2 minutes at medium speed in mixer. Scrape bowl occasionally. Add 3 eggs, egg white, and ½ cup flour to make a thick batter. Beat 2 minutes at high speed. Fold in raisins. Scrape bowl and stir in enough flour to make a soft dough. Turn out onto a lightly floured board. Knead until smooth and elastic, about 10 minutes. Place in a greased bowl and turn to grease top. Cover and let rise in a warm place until double in bulk, approximately 1 hour. Punch dough down and turn onto lightly floured board. Divide dough in half. Shape each half into a long coil, then wind upward to form a circle. Do the same with the other half. Place on greased cookie sheets. Beat remaining egg yolk with water and brush on loaves. If omitting raisins, sprinkle on 2 tablespoons poppy or sesame seed, if desired. Leave uncovered to rise until double, approximately 1 hour. Bake at 375 degrees F for 30 to 35 minutes or until golden brown on top.

Makes 2 loaves.

Autumn Vegetable Soup.

Sweet and Sour Meatballs

Meatballs
- 2 pounds lean ground shoulder steak
- ½ cup bread crumbs or matzah meal
- ⅓ cup water
- 2 eggs, lightly beaten
- 4 tablespoons fresh or 1 tablespoon dried minced onion
- ¼ teaspoon garlic powder
- 1 teaspoon salt
- ¼ teaspoon pepper
- ⅛ teaspoon allspice (optional)

Combine ingredients and shape into small meatballs. Set aside.

Sweet and Sour Sauce
- 3 cans (8 ounces each) tomato sauce
- ⅓ cup sugar
- 3 tablespoons lemon juice
- 1 cup water
- 1 onion, diced
- ½ green pepper, diced
- ⅓ cup raisins (optional)

Combine ingredients in a large saucepan. Bring to a boil. Add meatballs. Reduce heat, cover, and simmer for 45 minutes.

Serves 8.

Note: For stronger sweet and sour taste, increase lemon juice to ¼ cup and sugar to ½ cup.

Autumn Vegetable Soup

This vegetable soup is nutritious and delicious—a perfect beginning for a healthy New Year.

- 2 to 3 tablespoons olive oil
- 2 medium potatoes
- 1 yellow crook-necked squash
- 1 small zucchini
- 1 leek
- 2 parsnips
- 2 carrots
- 2 celery stalks
- 1 small onion
- 1 small white turnip or ¼ rutabaga
- ½ cup frozen peas (optional)
- 6 cups vegetable stock or broth
- 4 sprigs fresh dill
- 4 sprigs parsley
- Salt to taste
- Pepper to taste

Dice vegetables. Heat oil and sauté vegetables for several minutes until all vegetables are coated. Add stock or broth, dill, and parsley. Bring to a boil. Reduce heat, cover, and simmer for 20 minutes, until vegetables are soft. Taste and adjust seasoning with salt and pepper. Remove herb sprigs. Garnish with additional sprigs of fresh dill.

Serves 8.

Mixed Green Salad with Raspberry Vinaigrette Dressing

A blend of different greens with a sweet raspberry dressing for a sweet New Year.

- 1 small head Boston lettuce
- 1 head green or red leaf lettuce
- 1 small head radicchio
- 1 bunch watercress
- 1 bunch arugula
- 2 Belgian endives
- 1 14-ounce can hearts of palm, drained (optional)

Wash each green, drain, and dry. Tear lettuces and radicchio into small pieces. Tear stems from watercress and arugula. Slice endives crosswise or cut lengthwise into slivers. In large bowl, toss all ingredients together and refrigerate.

Serve on individual plates with hearts of palm and raspberry vinaigrette dressing on top. Garnish with raspberries.

Serves 8.

Raspberry Vinaigrette Dressing

- 1 10½ ounce package frozen raspberries in syrup, thawed
- 3 tablespoons raspberry or cider vinegar
- ⅓ to ½ cup vegetable oil (optional: part walnut oil)
- ¼ teaspoon salt
- ⅛ teaspoon cinnamon

Drain and reserve syrup from raspberries and set aside 3 to 4 tablespoons of raspberries for garnish. Combine remainder of raspberries with ¼ cup of raspberry syrup in a blender or food processor and puree until smooth. Strain raspberry puree through a fine sieve to remove seeds; discard seeds. Blend strained puree with vinegar, oil, salt, and cinnamon. Serve on top of mixed green salad.

Glazed Turkey Breast

This dish looks beautiful for the holidays. Stuff it with your favorite stuffing or cook the stuffing separately for vegetarians. A turkey breast comes either with the ribs or deboned. Boneless turkey breasts are particularly elegant when stuffed.

- 1 4- to 6-pound fresh turkey breast
- Half a lemon
- Seasoned salt
- 1 tablespoon pareve margarine
- ¼ cup dry white wine (optional)

Glaze
- ⅓ cup apricot or peach all-fruit spread
- 1 tablespoon lemon juice, dry white wine, or sherry
- 1½ tablespoons soy sauce
- 1 garlic clove, minced
- ½ teaspoon ginger, minced
- 1 teaspoon chives

Preheat oven to 325 degrees F. Clean and rinse turkey breast in cold water. Pat dry. Rub half a lemon over turkey, sprinkle with a little seasoned salt, and brush with a little margarine. Place turkey skin-side up. Insert meat thermometer into center of turkey breast and add wine if desired. Baste occasionally. Roast for about 1½ to 2 hours, or until meat thermometer registers 170 degrees F or juices run clear. Do not overcook. Allow about 22 minutes per pound.

Combine apricot or peach spread, lemon juice, soy sauce, garlic, ginger, and chives. Brush over turkey during last half hour of cooking. Let rest 15 minutes before serving. Cut crosswise and serve with skimmed turkey juices.

Serves 8 to 10.

Note: A less sweet glaze can be made by combining ⅓ cup dry white wine, 2 tablespoons water, 2 teaspoons cornstarch, 1½ tablespoons soy sauce, and 2 tablespoons honey in a saucepan. Cook until thick and clear.

Mixed Green Salad with Raspberry Vinaigrette Dressing.

Savory Couscous

Couscous (semolina) is a popular grain among Moroccan Jews. It is nutritious and light and can be used as a rice substitute. This recipe complements the turkey breast nicely. It takes but a few minutes to make.

- 2 tablespoons olive oil
- ¾ cup chopped scallions, including some of the green tops
- 2 large garlic cloves, minced
- 2½ cups boiling water, or chicken stock brought to a boil
- Freshly ground pepper
- ½ teaspoon salt
- 1¼ teaspoons cumin
- 1¼ teaspoons cinnamon
- 1 teaspoon ground coriander (optional)
- 1½ cups quick-cooking couscous
- 2 tablespoons lemon juice
- ¼ cup chopped fresh parsley
- 1 teaspoon marjoram (optional)
- ¼ to ⅓ cup shelled, unsalted pistachio nuts, pine nuts, or slivered almonds

Heat oil in a saucepan over medium heat. Add scallions and garlic and cook over medium heat. Stir until soft and translucent, but not brown, about 2 minutes. Add water or stock, pepper, salt, cumin, cinnamon, and coriander, and bring to a boil. Remove from heat and add couscous, lemon juice, parsley, marjoram, and nuts. Adjust seasoning. Cover and let stand 5 minutes. Uncover and fluff with a fork. Heat through before serving.

Serves 8.

Cranberry Applesauce

A delicious change from regular cranberry sauce. Freeze bags of cranberries when in season so you can use them year-round.

- 4 cups apples
- 2 cups cranberries
- ¾ cup water
- ⅔ to ¾ cup sugar

Peel and slice apples. Combine remaining ingredients and put into a pot with the apples. Bring to a boil, cover, reduce heat, and simmer about 10 minutes or until tender. Blend until smooth and fluffy.

Serves 8.

Rosh Hashanah main dish: Sliced Glazed Turkey Breast, Carrot Tzimmes, Savory Couscous, and Cranberry Applesauce.

Carrot Tzimmes

These sweet carrots, which resemble small coins, express the hope for a prosperous year.

- 1½ pounds carrots
- ½ cup water
- 1½ tablespoons lemon juice
- ½ teaspoon salt
- 2 tablespoons pareve margarine
- 1 tablespoon cornstarch
- ½ cup orange juice
- 3 tablespoons honey
- ¾ teaspoon powdered ginger
- ⅓ cup yellow raisins or chopped dried apricots (optional)

Scrape carrots and slice in ¼-inch rounds. Place in a heavy saucepan with water, lemon juice, salt, and margarine. Cover tightly and simmer until carrots are just tender, about 12 to 15 minutes. Meanwhile, blend cornstarch with orange juice, honey, and ginger. Remove carrots from liquid with slotted spoon. Stir orange juice mixture into carrot water and cook until thickened, stirring constantly. Return carrots to sauce, add raisins or apricots, and serve.

Serves 8.

Deluxe Honey Cake

This honey cake has a spicy but delicate flavor. It can be glazed with a honey or sugar glaze or decorated with pecan halves pressed on top of the batter before baking.

- ¾ cup vegetable oil
- 3 eggs
- ½ cup sugar
- 1 cup honey (preferably dark)
- 1 teaspoon grated orange or lemon rind
- 2 or 3 tablespoons orange or lemon juice
- 2 tablespoons brandy
- 3 cups flour (sifted if finer texture is desired)
- 1½ teaspoons baking powder
- 1 teaspoon baking soda
- ½ teaspoon salt
- 1 teaspoon cinnamon
- ½ teaspoon ginger
- ½ teaspoon nutmeg
- ½ teaspoon cloves
- ⅔ cup strong cold coffee
- ½ cup raisins
- ¼ cup chopped dried fruit tidbits or diced candied fruit (optional)
- ½ cup pecans, chopped
- Pecan halves for top

Glaze

- ½ cup sugar
- 2 tablespoons orange or lemon juice

or

- 3 tablespoons warm honey

Preheat oven to 350 degrees F. Grease a 10-inch tube pan or spray with a nonstick coating.

Beat together oil, eggs, sugar, honey, orange or lemon rind, orange or lemon juice, and brandy. Combine dry ingredients and add to honey mixture, alternating with coffee. Beat well. Fold in dried fruit and chopped pecans. Press pecan halves on top if not using glaze. Bake in preheated oven 50 to 60 minutes or until wooden toothpick inserted into center comes out clean. Cool in pan for 15 minutes. Remove from pan. While still warm, poke several holes on top of cake and pour warm sugar or honey glaze over the top.

To prepare sugar glaze: combine orange juice and sugar and bring to a simmer over medium heat. Stir just until sugar melts. Sugar glaze can also be made by simply combining sugar and juice without heating.

Serves 12.

Poached Pears with a dollop of Honey Cream.

Poached Pears in Wine Sauce

These pears are seasonal for Rosh Hashanah and make a light and delicious dessert after a heavy holiday meal. The reduced wine sauce imparts a lovely red color to the fruit. The liquid can be saved and used again. The best pears for poaching are Bosc, Bartlett, Anjou, and Comice. The wine loses its alcohol during the cooking process, but you can also try poaching pears in cranberry juice or cranraspberry juice (32 ounces) and cutting sugar to ⅓ cup.

- 8 pears, ripe and firm
- 1½ cups semidry red wine
- Water to cover pears
- Juice of half a lemon
- ¾ to 1 cup sugar
- 1 or 2 sticks cinnamon
- 1 small vanilla bean
- 2 teaspoons grated lemon rind

Peel pears, leave on stem, and set aside or keep in water. In a saucepan just large enough to hold the pears, combine wine, water, lemon juice, sugar, cinnamon stick, vanilla bean, and lemon rind. Bring to a boil. Gently add peeled pears and simmer for 10 to 15 minutes, until tender throughout, but not too soft. Lift gently with spatula and place in an attractive bowl. Reduce wine sauce in half by boiling. Cool 5 minutes. Strain and pour over pears. Refrigerate. Serve in individual dishes with sauce from bowl. Garnish with a dollop of honey cream (see recipe below).

Serves 8.

Honey Cream

- 8-ounce container nondairy topping
- 3 tablespoons honey
- 1 tablespoon brandy
- ½ teaspoon lemon extract

Defrost nondairy topping if frozen. In a medium-size bowl, whip topping until stiff. Add honey slowly and beat until stiff. Gently fold in brandy and lemon extract. Serve on top of honey cake or poached pears.

Sugar and Spice Cookies

- ½ cup pareve sweet margarine, room temperature
- ¾ cup sugar
- 1 egg
- 1 tablespoon nondairy creamer or apple juice
- 1¼ cups flour
- ¼ teaspoon salt
- ½ teaspoon baking powder
- ½ teaspoon cinnamon
- ½ teaspoon nutmeg
- ¼ teaspoon ginger
- ½ cup currants or raisins

Preheat oven to 325 degrees F. Cream margarine with sugar, and mix well. Add egg and creamer; mix until fluffy. Stir in dry ingredients, mixing thoroughly. Add currants or raisins. Drop onto greased cookie sheets and flatten with a fork. Bake 12 to 15 minutes or until lightly browned.

Makes 2½ dozen cookies.

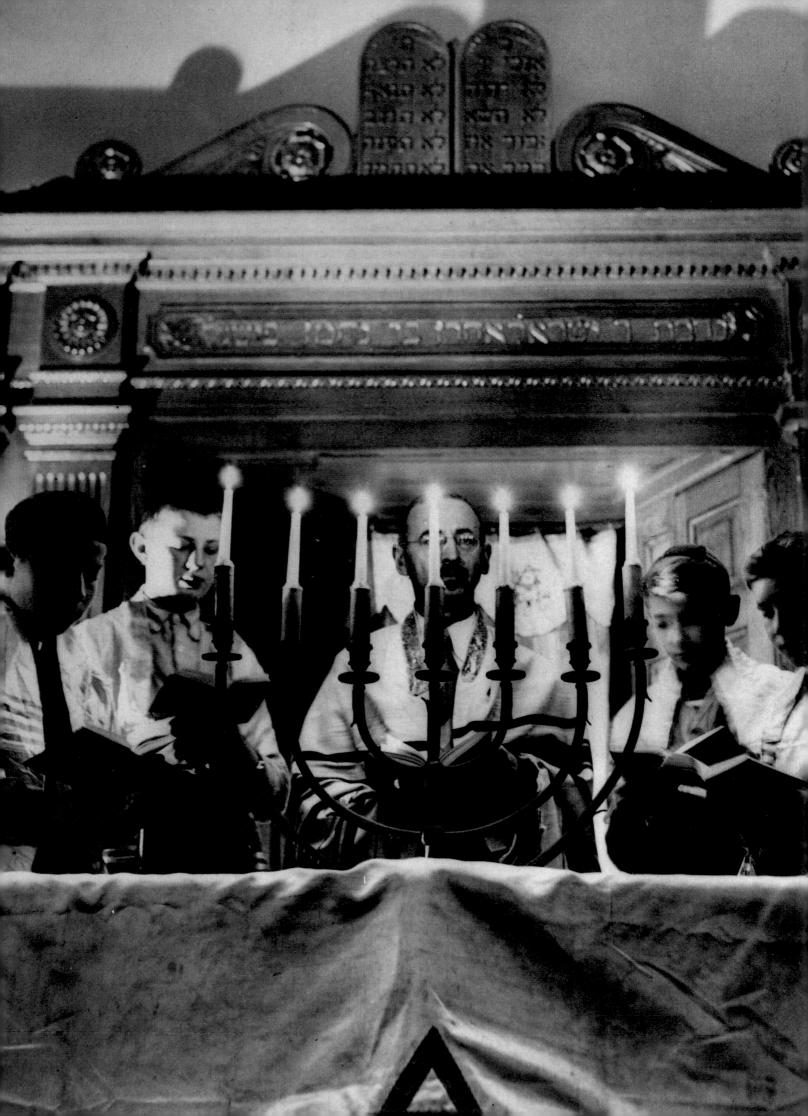

CHAPTER TWO

YOM KIPPUR

The climax of the High Holy Day season is the Sabbath of Sabbaths, the holiest day of the Jewish calendar, the Day of Atonement, Yom Kippur. Yom Kippur is a day suffused with awe and solemnity. Even Jews who otherwise do not attend services throughout the year often do so on Yom Kippur. Yom Kippur is the day of spiritual reckoning, when Jews come face-to-face with themselves and their creator through fasting, prayer, and meditation.

Yom Kippur is explicitly referred to in the Bible as a day of atonement and self-denial (Lev. 23:27,32). It was on Yom Kippur that the Jubilee year (see page 13), which occurred once every fifty years, was announced. Like Rosh Hashanah, Yom Kippur has gone through an evolution. Some scholars think that at one time the autumn holidays that are now Rosh Hashanah, Yom Kippur, and Sukkot were one long festive period, and only later were they broken into individual holidays.

During the period of the Second Temple, Yom Kippur was a great festival highlighted by the once-a-year ritual of the high priest dressed in simple white linen garb entering the holy of the holies of the Temple to utter God's ineffable name—the Tetragrammaton. That Yom Kippur also may have once been a more joyous festival

is hinted at in the Talmud with an unusual practice—young maidens dressed in white going out on the afternoon of Yom Kippur to dance in the vineyards of Jerusalem in search of appropriate mates. Yom Kippur was once known as *Yoma Rabbah*—the Great Day—later shortened to *Yoma*, meaning The Day. Yom Kippur is still the most important day of the Jewish calendar.

Opposite: Rabbi Dr. Ezekiel Landau leads four displaced persons in a Yom Kippur service at the Hebrew Immigrant Aid Society (HIAS). Right: A rabbi wearing a tallit, or prayer shawl, over his head pores over a sacred text. A tallit is worn at night only on Yom Kippur.

KOL NIDREI*

Kol nid - rei ve-e -sa rei u -sh' -vu-ei va-cha-ra-
mei- v' -ko -na mei v' -ki- nu - sei v' -chi -nu -yei
din - - dar - na u - d' - ish - ta -
va - na u - d' - a - cha - ri - m'na u - d' - a - sar-
na al naf - sha - ta -na.

All vows, oaths, and promises to God with which we obligate
ourselves shall be annulled.

*See music on page 116.

KOL NIDREI

The eve of Yom Kippur, which is known as *Kol Nidrei*, takes its name from the most famous "prayer" of all, the *Kol Nidrei*, and ushers in the Day of Atonement.

So famous was the *Kol Nidrei* chant that even non-Jews in Europe would gather outside synagogues to catch a few notes of its haunting and stirring melody. Max Bruch, a non-Jewish composer, and Arnold Schoenberg both wrote symphonic compositions based on the *Kol Nidrei*. Michael Erdenko, a Russian composer, is said to have played his rendition for Leo Tolstoy, who thought the *Kol Nidrei* to be the saddest but most uplifting of all melodies.

THE KOL NIDREI PRAYER

No prayer in the entire Jewish liturgy is as well known or has as powerful a hold on the emotional and spiritual imagination as the *Kol Nidrei*. Even the most estranged Jews have felt the spiritual tug of the *Kol Nidrei* and have found their way into the synagogue to listen and sometimes weep. The *Kol Nidrei* prayer, however, had a controversial and contentious beginning.

The origin of the *Kol Nidrei* prayer, subject to much scholarly research, is still shrouded in mystery. By the eighth century C.E.—often against the vociferous objections of rabbinic leaders and authorities—Jews began to recite this prayer, which annuls all rash vows made by individuals and communities. By the tenth century, the *Kol Nidrei* became a standard part of the opening liturgy of Yom Kippur, the Day of Atonement. And by the twelfth century, the wording had been changed to include only those rash vows that would be made in the year to come. Today, Sephardic communities still retain the older wording, which refers to vows made in the past year. Currently, Ashkenazic Jews refer to future vows, while Sephardic Jews and Ashkenazic Jews living in Israel refer to both.

The prayer itself is dry and devoid of drama. Written in Aramaic, it hardly seems like the kind of piece that would engender so much passion and power. Some scholars suggest that it is the music that invests the *Kol Nidrei* with so much force. But that does not explain why the prayer carries so much weight in communities where this piece of music, so beautifully arranged by the non-Jewish composer Max Bruch, is unknown.

Perhaps the mystery lies not only in its place as the opening chord of the Yom Kippur service, but in the idea that speech is the gift that separates human beings from other creatures. Speech comes as close to the Divine character as is possible.

Thus, the *Kol Nidrei* becomes a powerful reminder of the Godly and spiritual within, and a terrible reminder of how often words fail us, and we fail the words we speak.

A Kol Nidrei *service at Temple Beth Or, Everett, Washington.*

The *Kol Nidrei* itself is not a prayer, but a legal formula written in Aramaic—the language of the people—to nullify vows made rashly or unwittingly. This refers to vows made to one's conscience or to God, but not to vows made between two human beings.

The meal before the *Kol Nidrei* service is known as the *seudah mafseket* ("the closing meal"). Usually, it consists of bland food in order to prepare for the coming fast. The Yom Kippur fast is a twenty-five-hour fast lasting from before sundown to after sundown the next day. According to the sages, just as it is incumbent upon Jews to fast on Yom Kippur, so should they eat heartily before the Yom Kippur fast, in order to give themselves over completely to the spiritual needs of the day. There is a Hasidic tale about a rabbi who said, "Our eating on the day before Yom Kippur is more worthy than our fasting on Yom Kippur, because by eating, we show our faith that God will forgive our sins." The meal must be concluded while it is still daylight, to allow enough time to go to synagogue to hear the *Kol Nidrei*, which must begin before sunset.

A prayer shawl, or tallit, worn by the men, and in some congregations by women as well, is donned before the start of the *Kol Nidrei* service while it is still daylight and worn throughout Yom Kippur. A tallit is never worn at night, but an exception is made on Yom Kippur because Jews are considered as angels without earthly needs.

Before the actual *Kol Nidrei* formula is recited, sinners, or *avaryanim*, are asked to rejoin the community. *"By authority of the court on high and by authority of this court below, we hereby declare that it is permitted to pray with those who have transgressed."* Some think that the transgressors referred to in this declaration were excommunicated Jews and that this part of the text dates to the thirteenth century. It is also suggested that the word *avaryanim* could be a play on the word "Iberian" and that this declaration was an invitation to Marranos, who were forcibly converted to Catholicism during the Spanish Inquisition, to rejoin their brethren on Yom Kippur.

The *Kol Nidrei* formula is recited three times—each time more loudly than the previous time—with all the scrolls of the law removed from the ark. The service reader is flanked by two persons holding Torahs, which constitutes a court of law because absolution of vows was done before a court. Thus, the synagogue itself is transformed into a court of law. The *Kol Nidrei* is recited before sundown, while the sun is still on the horizon, because court is in session during the day, not at night or on a holiday.

CONFESSIONAL

There is a special *nusah*, or liturgical melody, used in the service on Yom Kippur eve. Among the distinctive features of the service is the confessional, or *vidui*, which is recited no fewer than ten times before Yom Kippur is over. The confessional is always recited in the plural, emphasizing communal responsibility.

The first part of the confessional, the *ashamnu* ("we have sinned"), is written in alphabetic acrostic, while the second part, the *al het* ("for the sin"), also alphabetical, is more specific. A sin, in the Jewish tradition, is a missing of the mark, a form of alienation from God, with the remedy or antidote being sincere repentance and atonement. To atone with the idea of repeating one's transgressions is unacceptable. Repentance and atonement

AVINU MALKEINU*

Andante religioso
Liturgy Folksong

A - vi-nu mal - kei - nu cha nei nu va - a - nei -
nu— a - vi-nu mal - kei - nu cha - nei - nu va - a - nei - nu ki
ein ba - nu ma - a - sim— a - sei - i - ma nu - tz' - da ka
va - che - sed — a - sei i - ma - nu tz'- da - ka va - che - sed
v' - ho - shi - ei — nu

Our Father, our King, be gracious unto us and answer us. Although unworthy, deal with us in charity and loving kindness and save us.

*See music on page 116.

RESTRICTIONS FOR THE DAY OF ATONEMENT

All restrictions of Shabbat and more apply to Yom Kippur. No food or drink (even when Yom Kippur falls on Shabbat), except for children under bar or bat mitzvah age and for persons who are too ill to fast or in physical danger.

- No anointing or washing of the body.

- No sexual relations, as that is considered pleasure.

- No wearing of leather shoes, because leather is considered a luxury, and, according to one medieval rabbi, one should not wear the skin of another creature when asking for forgiveness.

- Earthly needs are abandoned on Yom Kippur and replaced by spiritual yearnings.

require remorse, change of behavior, and a determination not to repeat one's offenses.

In the *al het*, the sins of speech are especially emphasized, for the Rabbis thought that these sins were among the most serious of transgressions. Some of the sins of speech enumerated are falsifying, mocking, jeering, insulting, lying, and slander. The Talmud says that the sin of slander kills three people: the one who says it, the one who hears it, and the one about whom the slander is spoken.

YOM KIPPUR LITURGY

The entire day of Yom Kippur is spent in the synagogue, devoted to meditation and prayer, many of them prayers of atonement with an appeal to Divine mercy and a return to grace. There are five distinct services on the Day of Atonement:

Ma'ariv including *Kol Nidrei*; *Shaharit*; *Musaf*; *Minhah*; and *Ne'ilah*. During the morning Torah reading, six people (seven if Yom Kippur falls on Shabbat) are honored by being called to the Torah (instead of the usual seven for Shabbat and five for other festivals). The Torah reading deals with the form and ritual of the sacrifices, while the Haftarah (the prophetic reading following the Torah) comes from the Book of Isaiah, and deals with spirit and substance, emphasizing that the purpose of the fast is to become a more caring and sensitive person, to abandon evil, and to look after the less fortunate and help the oppressed.

The *Musaf*, or additional service, is the highlight of this day of prayer. Particular to the *Musaf* service is the elaborate pageantry described in the *Avodah* service: a detailed verbal reenactment of the sacrificial service in the days of the Temple. The High Priest, changing clothes five times, would perform the expiation rites and send a scapegoat off into the wilderness, symbolically carrying away with it the sins of the people of Israel.

A woman rabbi reads from the Torah. Today many synagogues are egalitarian and women fully participate in Jewish religious life.

Another outstanding feature of the *Musaf* service is the *Eleh Ezkerah* (martyrology). This portion of the service recalls ten great Jewish scholars and sages who were cruelly tortured to death by the Romans during the Hadrianic period (115–138 C.E.) because of their teaching of Torah. The actual martyrology took place at different times, not simultaneously, as implied by the text. At this point in many synagogues, Holocaust poems and memoirs are also incorporated into the service to appeal to Divine mercy by demonstrating Jewish sacrifice and the courage required for survival.

A special memorial service for the departed, known as *Yizkor*, is recited on Yom Kippur and other festivals.

The *Minhah*, or afternoon service, is a short service. The highlight of this service is the reading of the entire Book of Jonah

ON THE DAY OF ATONEMENT

by Yehuda Amichai

On the Day of Atonement in 1967, I put on my dark holiday suit and went to the Old City in Jerusalem. I stood, for some time, before the alcove of an Arab's shop, not far from Damascus Gate, a shop of buttons and zippers and spools of thread in all colours, and snaps and buckles. A glorious light and a great many colours like a Holy Ark with its doors ajar.

I told him in my heart that my father, too, had such a shop of threads and buttons. I explained to him in my heart all about the tens of years and the reasons and the circumstances because of which I am now here and my father's shop is in ashes there, and he is buried here.

By the time I had finished, it was the hour of 'the locking of the Gates'. He too pulled down the shutter and locked the gate, and I went back home with all the worshippers.

THE STORY OF FRANZ ROSENZWEIG

Franz Rosenzweig, born in 1886, was the son of largely assimilated German Jewish parents. Because Judaism was meaningless to him, and most of his relatives had converted to Christianity, Rosenzweig decided to do likewise. However, he was determined to do so not as a pagan, but as a Jew.

On October 11, 1913, he decided to attend services for the last time on Yom Kippur at an Orthodox synagogue in Berlin. It was an experience that would change his life. Rosenzweig was transformed on that fateful Yom Kippur day. He found meaning in that service that had until then eluded him—it was an epiphany. He rediscovered his own buried Jewish soul and began to see Judaism not as a dead religion, but as a faith for the living. No longer feeling the need to convert, Rosenzweig embarked upon a journey to reclaim his heritage. He studied with some of the important scholars of his day, and went on to become one of the greatest Jewish theologians and thinkers of all time.

Franz Rosenzweig had this comment on the practice of kneeling, called *kor'im*, which is done only in the *Aleinu* prayer in the *Musaf* service on High Holy Days: "What distinguishes the Days of Awe from all other festivals is that here and only here does the Jew kneel. Here he does what he refused to do before the King of Persia, what no power on earth can compel him to do, and what he need not do before God on any other day of the year, or in any other situation he may face during his lifetime.

"And he does not kneel to confirm a fault or to pray for forgiveness of sins, acts to which this festival is primarily dedicated. He kneels only on beholding the immediate nearness of God, hence on an occasion which transcends the earthly needs of today."

Franz Rosenzweig (1886–1929).

THE STORY OF JONAH

The Book of Jonah is as much a study in contrast as it is a description of a reluctant prophet. It is a story about a caring, compassionate, and loving God who loves His creatures and immediately accepts their contrition for their sins. It is also the story about a detached, remote, and distant man who tries to run away from the merciful God, and runs into himself, remaining alone and aloof.

Told by God that he is to book passage to the great city of Ninevah, capital of Assyria, to warn the people of their impending destruction if they do not repent and atone for their wicked and unjust ways, Jonah flees to a faraway place called Tarshish.

While Jonah sleeps in the bowels of a ship, a dangerous storm threatens to tear the vessel apart. Jonah is oblivious.

After being awakened by the captain of the ship, Jonah tells the deck hands that he is responsible for the storm, and the only way that they will survive is to throw him overboard. Jonah is cast into the sea and swallowed by a big fish.

Here we have a narrative about a man in a personal state of numbness: he is numb to God's message, and he is numb to the perilous state of the vessel and its passengers.

From the big fish, however, Jonah prays to God to be delivered from his own imprisonment. God hears Jonah's plea and he is spewed forth onto the shoreline. He makes his way to Ninevah to fulfill God's command. As he walks through the city, his voice is heard and the people of the great city listen and repent. But Jonah develops no relationship with any of its inhabitants. He leaves and takes up his position outside the city to see what happens. He remains physically and emotionally detached. At the same time, Jonah also sees that God is anxious about the inhabitants of the city and has put aside harsh judgment for mercy and compassion. Jonah is displeased.

As he watches to see what becomes of the city, a quick-growing plant provides shade: a cocoon that protects Jonah from sun and wind, night and cold. He is content. In the morning, a worm kills the plant, and Jonah is subject to a terrible, dry wind. He becomes so unhappy that he wishes for death: the final isolation and detachment.

When he is asked by God why he is so unhappy about the death of the plant, Jonah responds by saying, in effect, that he does not want to be vulnerable or responsible, not to nature, not to man, not to God. God tells Jonah that caring and compassion is a Divine and human responsibility and all life demands consideration for its own sake. A true soul has regard for all of God's creations. Despite God's admonition, the lingering image left with the reader is Jonah alone at the edge of the city.

The message of the book, then, is that as Yom Kippur draws to a close, we learn that God is the Master of all humanity and that He has regard for all people. God's love, though not unconditional, is easy to awaken, and His compassion is near and always imminent, as long as one atones and repents.

from the prophets. Jonah is read to demonstrate that the power of repentance and forgiveness is not limited to Jews alone, but extends to all God's people, reiterating the belief that God's mercy and love are universal. Jonah was sent on a mission to change the ways of the residents of the city of Ninevah, an Assyrian city. Although Jonah himself was a recalcitrant and uncompassionate messenger, his message of repentance was a compelling one that brought results and therefore is in keeping with the Yom Kippur themes of repentance, atonement, mercy, and forgiveness.

Yom Kippur ends with the *Ne'ilah* service, which is now unique to Yom Kippur. *Ne'ilah* refers to the *ne'ilat shearim*—the closing of the ancient Temple gates—but metaphorically, it also means the closing of the gates of heaven. As such, *Ne'ilah* takes on the urgency of a final appeal. Prayers that ended with "remember us unto life" now close with "seal us unto life." Many people stand throughout the *Ne'ilah* service because the ark remains open, emphasizing *Ne'ilah*'s importance as the Yom Kippur day is waning.

The end of *Ne'ilah*, which completes the Yom Kippur fast, is signaled by one long uninterrupted blast of the shofar and the call of "Next Year in Jerusalem." In Israel, the call is "Next year in (spiritually) rebuilt Jerusalem." The mood is decidedly upbeat, and the High Holy Day season, which began with such seriousness of purpose, has taken its adherents through a specific and prescribed cathartic process of spiritual renewal, ending on a high note.

TRADITIONS AND CUSTOMS ASSOCIATED WITH YOM KIPPUR

- Giving charity before Yom Kippur begins.
- Some pious Jews go to purify themselves in the mikvah, the ritual bath, before Yom Kippur.
- *Kapparot* is a controversial custom that was frowned upon by many rabbis and is no longer done much. It entails swinging a live rooster (for a male) or a hen (for a female) over one's head as a substitute for oneself in a symbolic transfer of sin (like a scapegoat). The fowl is then slaughtered and given to the poor. Money placed in a handkerchief in the same ceremony came to substitute for the fowl.
- Eating well before Yom Kippur to prepare for the fast and honor the day, since it is forbidden by Jewish law to eat and drink from before sunset of Yom Kippur until after sunset the next day.
- Blessing the children before leaving for the synagogue with the following: For girls, "May you be like Sarah, Rebekah, Rachel, and Leah." For boys, "May you be like Ephraim and Menasseh." In many families, this prayer is said every Shabbat eve, but for some, it is specifically reserved for *Kol Nidrei* eve.

- Wearing of white clothing for women and a *kittel* (a white robe) for men (and nowadays some women as well). White is a symbol of purity. A *kittel* is also worn before entering a new state, such as matrimony, and Yom Kippur can be thought of as entering a new dimension. Symbolic of a shroud, a *kittel* is also a reminder of one's mortality.
- Wearing shoes of man-made material instead of leather, such as sneakers.
- Lighting memorial candles (Yahrzeit lights) for departed relatives before leaving for synagogue on *Kol Nidrei* eve.
- Driving the first nail into the sukkah immediately after the fast, to return to the normal rhythm of Jewish life and begin a mitzvah (commandment) with the new vigor and sense of purpose achieved by the Days of Awe.

Hiddur Mitzah (Enhancing the Holiday)

Give generously to a favorite charity before Yom Kippur, especially one concerned with social causes. *Tzedakah*, an act of righteousness (charity), is a cornerstone of the Jewish value system. Acquiring an attractive *tzedakah* box may serve as a daily reminder that this important mitzvah and good deed is not limited to Yom Kippur, but should be performed regularly.

Wearing white for Yom Kippur is a time-honored tradition that reflects the spirit and mood of the day. Wear or acquire a special piece of white clothing—a dress, suit, blouse, shirt, or even a white yarmulke, or head covering.

Polish Jews on Yom Kippur in prayer and meditation. This print portrays Jewish life in Poland as it once was.

A meatless or dairy buffet is often served after Yom Kippur for the break-the-fast. Deviled eggs and marinated tomatoes are shown.

YOM KIPPUR BREAK-THE-FAST MENU

The menu for the break-the-fast meal is usually dairy and contains a variety of dishes which can be served buffet-style. Fresh juice, cheese, fish, bagels, kugels, and salads are customary fare.

Orange Juice
*Spinach Kugel
Fish Platter: Gefilte Fish, Smoked Carp, White Fish Salad, Lox, *Herring Salad
Cheese Platter: Cream Cheese, Cheese Spreads, Assorted Hard Cheeses
Salads: *Dill Cucumber Salad, *Marinated Tomatoes, *Health Salad
*Hummus
*Deviled Eggs
Bread: Bagels, Rolls, Crackers, Pita Bread
Desserts: *Apple Tart, *Light Strawberry Mousse,
*Mocha Walnut Chiffon Cake, *Butter Almond Toffee Bars
Fruit Platter: Melons, Mangoes, Pineapple, Kiwis

Spinach Kugel

A wonderful and nutritious kugel of cheese and spinach. This recipe is from my sister Laurie Gottlieb of Montreal, Canada.

- 1 12-ounce package medium egg noodles
- 2 tablespoons butter
- 1 large onion, chopped
- 1 10-ounce package chopped frozen spinach
- 4 eggs
- ½ pound dry cottage cheese or farmer cheese
- 4 ounces Gruyère or white cheddar cheese, shredded
- 1 cup milk
- 1 teaspoon salt
- ½ teaspoon pepper
- 2 teaspoons butter, melted
- 3 tablespoons seasoned bread crumbs

Preheat oven to 350 degrees F. Grease a 9- by 13-inch glass dish.

Boil a pot of water and cook noodles until slightly tender. Set aside. Melt butter and sauté onions until soft and translucent, about 5 minutes. Set aside. Cook spinach and squeeze out water.

Beat eggs. Add cottage or farmer cheese, Gruyère or cheddar cheese, milk, spinach, onions, and noodles. Season with salt and pepper. Pour into glass dish. Combine melted butter and bread crumbs. Spread on top of kugel. Bake for 40 minutes, or until the kugel is golden brown and firm.

Serves 8 to 10.

Herring Salad

My good friend Max Kaufmann gave me this recipe, which keeps especially well.

- 4 medium-size sweet onions (such as Vidalia)
- 4 tablespoons sugar
- 3 scallions, chopped
- 1 stalk celery, finely chopped
- 1 dill pickle, finely diced
- 1 red pepper, diced
- 1 2-pound jar herring tidbits in wine sauce
- 1 16-ounce container sour cream

Chop onions. Add sugar and set aside. Combine scallions, celery, pickle, and pepper. Drain liquid from herring and cut into smaller tidbits. Add herring to vegetables. Add onions. Let stand ½ hour. Drain liquid and add sour cream. Transfer to bowl and serve.

Serves 15.

Spinach Kugel.

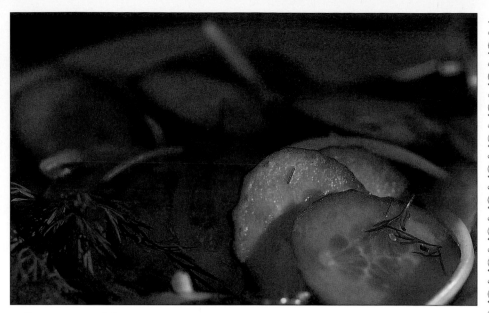

Dill Cucumber Salad.

Dill Cucumber Salad

White radishes add a nice crunch to this salad without discoloring it.

- 3 medium cucumbers, peeled, scored with a fork lengthwise, thinly sliced
- 1 Vidalia onion, thinly sliced
- ⅓ cup daikon (or other white) radishes, thinly sliced

Marinade
- ½ cup water
- ½ cup rice vinegar or white wine vinegar
- 3 tablespoons sugar
- 1 teaspoon salt
- ⅛ teaspoon pepper
- Fresh dill or dill weed, according to taste

Place cucumbers, onion, and radishes in a bowl. Combine water, vinegar, sugar, salt, and pepper, and mix well. Pour over cucumber salad and add dill. Cover and refrigerate for several hours. Drain marinade and serve.

Serves 8.

Marinated Tomatoes

The best tomatoes are from your garden or a local farmstand. The next best are Israeli tomatoes, internationally renowned for their uniformity and quality.

- 6 medium tomatoes, or 1½ pints of cherry tomatoes
- Italian seasoning or snips of fresh herbs (oregano, basil, marjoram, thyme, chervil)
- 1 teaspoon herbal salt-substitute seasoning
- Sprinkling of dried minced onion (optional)

Marinade
- 3 tablespoons red wine vinegar or balsamic vinegar
- 9 tablespoons olive oil
- ⅛ teaspoon pepper
- Salt to taste

Slice tomatoes (halve cherry tomatoes). Sprinkle with Italian seasoning or snips of fresh herbs, and herbal salt-substitute. Arrange on plate. Sprinkle with minced onion. Combine vinegar, oil, and pepper and shake until well blended. Drizzle over tomatoes. Cover and refrigerate. Lightly salt tomatoes before serving.

Serves 8.

Note: You can vary the recipe by substituting cilantro (fresh coriander) for the dried or fresh herbs. Equal parts of olive oil and lemon juice for the marinade can also be used.

Marinated Tomatoes.

Health Salad.

Health Salad

This imaginative recipe for health salad was created by my sister Linda Switkin of Columbus, Ohio.

- 1½ pounds green cabbage
- ½ pound red cabbage (optional)
- 3 carrots
- 1 yellow or red pepper
- 1 green pepper
- 1 large white onion
- 1 small red onion
- 2 cucumbers

Shred cabbage. Thinly slice carrots, peppers, onions, and cucumbers. Peppers may be cut into chunks. Combine in a large bowl and add marinade.

Marinade
- ½ cup white wine vinegar
- ⅓ cup vegetable oil
- 1 tablespoon fresh lemon juice
- 2 tablespoons water
- ⅓ cup sugar
- 1 tablespoon fresh parsley, finely chopped
- ½ teaspoon dill weed or 1 tablespoon fresh dill
- 2 teaspoons salt
- Pepper to taste

Combine all ingredients and blend well. Add to vegetables. Marinate 4 to 6 hours.
Serves 8 to 10.

Hummus

This popular Middle Eastern food is easy to make in one step in the food processor or blender.

- 1 15-ounce can chickpeas (garbanzo beans)
- 2 large garlic cloves, minced
- A few drops of Tabasco® sauce (optional)
- 1 teaspoon cumin
- ⅓ cup water
- Juice of 1 large lemon
- 6 tablespoons sesame tahini (available in health food-stores and some supermarkets)
- 1 teaspoon salt
- Pepper to taste

Drain chickpeas. Put all ingredients in a food processor and process until smooth. If too thick, add a little more water. Put in bowl or on plate and sprinkle with cayenne pepper, chopped parsley, and drizzle with a little olive oil. Serve with pita wedges.
Makes 1 cup.

Hummus served with Pita Bread.

Deviled Eggs.

Deviled Eggs

- 6 hard-boiled eggs, shelled
- 3 tablespoons mayonnaise or salad dressing
- 2 teaspoons lemon juice
- ½ teaspoon dry mustard
- ¼ teaspoon salt
- 2 teaspoons chives
- 2 teaspoons drained capers (optional)
- Paprika

Cut eggs in half lengthwise and remove yolks. Mash yolks well with fork. Add rest of ingredients to the yolks and mash until very smooth. Fill egg whites with yolk mixture and sprinkle tops with paprika.

Makes 12 halves.

Apple Tart

A fluted flan or tart pan has a removable bottom, which makes a beautiful and attractive tart, although any 9-inch pie pan will do. The crust is not rolled, but pressed into the pan. The filling forms a lovely custard over the apples.

Crust
- 1¾ cups flour
- ¼ cup sugar
- ½ cup plus 2 tablespoons unsalted butter or margarine, in pieces
- Pinch of salt
- 2 egg yolks
- ¼ teaspoon vanilla
- 2 teaspoons lemon peel, grated

Filling
- ½ cup sugar
- ¼ cup flour
- 2 eggs
- ½ cup unsalted butter or margarine, melted and slightly brown
- 2 teaspoons grated lemon peel
- ¼ teaspoon vanilla
- 5 medium McIntosh or Golden Delicious apples, peeled and thinly sliced
- Confectioners' sugar

Preheat oven to 375 degrees F.

Crust: Put flour, sugar, butter or margarine, and salt in a food processor fitted with the steel blade and process, pulsing on and off until mixture resembles coarse meal, about 15 seconds; or cut margarine into flour by hand. Combine yolks, vanilla, and lemon peel, and add to dough through the feed tube as machine is running, for another 15 seconds, or mix by hand. Work with hands until dough comes together. Cover and let rest for 30 minutes or refrigerate until ready to use. When ready to fill, press dough into sides and bottom of tart pan. Chill until ready to use.

Filling: Combine sugar, flour, and eggs and beat until smooth. Stir in melted butter or margarine, lemon peel, and vanilla. Arrange apple slices on pie crust. Pour filling over apples and bake about 40 to 45 minutes or until golden brown. After tart has cooled, sift confectioners' sugar on top.

Serves 8.

Light Strawberry Mousse

My sister Linda adapted this mousse recipe from a denser mousse recipe I once gave her. It works equally well as a raspberry mousse using frozen raspberries and raspberry-flavored gelatin.

- 2 10-ounce packages frozen strawberries in light syrup
- 1 tablespoon lemon juice
- 1 3-ounce package strawberry-flavored gelatin
- 1½ cups whipping cream or nondairy topping
- 2 egg whites

Crush strawberries, drain, and reserve juice. To strawberry juice, add lemon juice and enough water to make 1½ cups liquid. In small saucepan, bring juice mixture to boil and dissolve gelatin. Remove from heat and cool. Add crushed strawberries. Place in bowl and refrigerate 15 to 20 minutes. Whip cream until it stands in soft peaks, and add to strawberry mixture. Beat egg whites until stiff but not dry. Gently fold into mixture. Pour into bowl or mold and refrigerate several hours or overnight. Garnish with fresh strawberries.

Serves 8 to 10.

Note: For a denser mousse, use 6 ounces strawberry-flavored gelatin and 1 pint whipping cream, and leave out egg whites.

Mocha Walnut Chiffon Cake

This is a special treat for coffee lovers. This cake can be used for both meat and dairy meals, as it is pareve.

- 1 cup flour
- ¾ cup sugar
- 1½ teaspoons baking powder
- ½ teaspoon salt
- ¼ cup vegetable oil
- 3 egg yolks
- ¼ cup plus 2 tablespoons cold water
- 1 teaspoon vanilla or walnut extract
- 4 egg whites
- ¼ teaspoon cream of tartar
- ½ cup walnuts, finely chopped

Preheat oven to 325 degrees F.

In bowl, combine flour, sugar, baking powder, and salt. Make a well in the center and add, in order, oil, egg yolks, water, and vanilla. Beat with a spoon until smooth. In a large bowl, beat egg whites and cream of tartar until very stiff peaks form. Pour yolk mixture over whites and fold in with rubber scraper until blended. Fold in walnuts. Pour into ungreased 9- by 5- by 3-inch loaf pan. Bake for 50 to 55 minutes or until a toothpick inserted into the center comes out clean. Invert and remove from pan when cool.

Mocha Butter Cream Icing
- 3 cups confectioners' sugar
- ⅓ cup softened margarine or butter
- 1 teaspoon vanilla
- 3 tablespoons coffee liqueur or 1 teaspoon instant coffee dissolved in 3 tablespoons warm water
- ½ teaspoon mocha extract (optional)

Garnish: walnut halves and chocolate coffee beans

Combine sugar and margarine or butter. Stir in liqueur and extracts. Beat until smooth and spreadable.

Spread on cake after it has been removed from pan and garnish with walnut halves and chocolate coffee beans.

Serves 8.

Butter Almond Toffee Bars

These luscious shortbread bars have nuts in both the crust and the top.

- ½ cup blanched slivered almonds
- 1 cup butter
- 1 cup brown sugar
- 1 teaspoon vanilla
- 1 egg yolk
- 2 cups flour
- ¼ teaspoon salt
- ½ cup finely chopped untoasted almonds
- 6 ounces milk chocolate or semi-sweet chocolate chips

Preheat oven to 350 degrees F. Grease or spray a 9- by 13-inch pan with nonstick coating. Toast ½ cup blanched slivered almonds for 8 minutes, or until lightly brown. Remove from oven and let cool. Mix butter, brown sugar, vanilla, and egg yolk until fluffy. Add flour, salt, and ½ cup untoasted chopped almonds. Press into greased pan. Bake about 25 minutes or until lightly browned. Remove from oven and immediately sprinkle with chocolate chips. Let melt and spread over cookie base. Cover with toasted almonds. Cool and cut into bars.

Makes 24 bars.

Note: Almonds may also be toasted in microwave for 3 minutes.

CHAPTER THREE

SUKKOT, SHEMINI ATZERET, AND SIMHAT TORAH

SUKKOT

A nineteenth-century Hasidic rabbi once observed that the outcome of holiness is joyfulness. Four days after Yom Kippur, the seven-day thanksgiving festival of booths, Hag Hasukkot, bursts upon the autumnal Jewish calendar with its mirth and gladness, a welcome contrast to the intensity of the High Holy Day period. There is a unique joy that comes from beginning the cycle of Jewish holidays anew, after having undergone the spiritual cleansing of the High Holy Days.

The first two days of Sukkot (which is observed for one day in Israel and for one day by Reform Jews everywhere) are *yom tov*—full sacred holidays when no work is done. The five intermediate days that follow are *Hol Hamoed*, or semiholidays, including the seventh day of Sukkot, known as Hoshana Rabbah. Appended to the end of Sukkot are the independent holidays of Shemini Atzeret and Simhat Torah (observed for one day in Israel and two days in the Diaspora), which some see as the eighth and ninth days of Sukkot and are likewise *yom tov*.

"And you shall rejoice in your festivals" is written in the Book of Deuteronomy in reference to the holiday of Sukkot. Sukkot commemorates the time when the Israelites built temporary dwellings as they wandered in the wilderness. In the Bible, Sukkot

Opposite: Thousands of worshippers gather at the Western Wall to commemorate Sukkot, the Festival of Tabernacles. Near the wall are Kohanim (priests) with tallitot over their heads performing the traditional priestly blessing. Left: This early-twentieth-century photo shows the joy of the festival of Sukkot reflected on the faces of these women and girls.

was the most joyous and celebrated of festivals. In Jewish liturgy, Sukkot is described as *zeman simhateinu*—the time of our rejoicing.

When the Israelites lived in their own land, Canaan, Sukkot was primarily an autumn harvest festival modeled upon the agricultural festivals of the ancient Canaanites, who were the indigenous population of the land at the time of the Israelite conquest. Another name for Sukkot was *Hag Haasif*—the time of the ingathering of harvest crops and fruit.

> In ancient times, after the year's final harvest, our people made the hard journey to Jerusalem to offer thanks for the blessing of fruit and grain, to share the harvest with the poor and needy, as they had been commanded.
>
> We too are commanded: the rich must give to the poor, the strong help the weak, and all live together in peace. And we have learned: not charity, but justice is demanded of us. We must so order society that all people may earn their daily bread with dignity.
>
> From The New Union Prayer Book, *Gates of Prayer*, © 1975 by the Central Conference of American Rabbis, and reprinted with their permission.

FEAST OF BOOTHS

This was a season of our fathers' joy:
not only when they gathered grapes and the fruit of trees in Israel,
but when, locked in the dark and stony streets,
they held—symbols of a life from which they were banished
but to which they would surely return—
the branches of palm trees and of willows, the twigs of the myrtle,
and the bright odorous citrons.

This was the grove of palms with its deep well
in the stony ghetto in the blaze of noon;
this the living stream lined with willows;
and this the thick-leaved myrtles and trees heavy with fruit
in the barren ghetto—a garden
where the unjustly hated were justly safe at last.

In booths this week of holiday
as those who gathered grapes in Israel lived
and also to remember we were cared for
in the wilderness—
I remember how frail my present dwelling is
even if of stones and steel.

I know this is the season of our joy:
we have completed the readings of the Law
and we begin again;
but I remember how slowly I have learnt, how little,
how fast the year went by, the years—how few.

"Feast of Booths" by Charles Reznikoff. © 1977 by Marie Syrkin Reznikoff. Reprinted from *Poems 1918–1975: The Complete Poems of Charles Reznikoff* with the permission of Black Sparrow Press.

During biblical times, until the end of the First Commonwealth in 586 B.C.E., Sukkot was celebrated with great revelry and abandon. It was so important a holiday that it became known simply as *Hehag,* or *the* festival.

Solomon's Temple was consecrated on Sukkot, underlining the holiday's significance as the major festival of that time. As one of three pilgrimage holidays (Passover and Shavuot being the others), Sukkot was the time when ancient Israelites would flock to Jerusalem bearing offerings of animals, grains, fruit, oil, and wine to the Temple, while dwelling in harvesters' huts nearby. Since Sukkot marked the end of the harvest festival and the agricultural year, thousands were able to take the time off to come to Jerusalem to celebrate and offer their thanksgiving.

So great was the joy generated by Sukkot that a special festivity became part of the holiday in Temple times. Vividly described in the Talmud and known as *Simhat Beit Hashoeivah*, it was the water-drawing celebration, in connection with the Temple rite of water libation. Water was drawn from Jerusalem's chief spring, the brook of Siloam, and poured upon the altar in a ceremonial appeal for plentiful rain, which was to begin at this season. The festivities took place every night of *Hol Hamoed* (the intermediate days of the holiday) in the women's courtyard of the Temple. Huge golden candelabras lit up all of Jerusalem. Great scholars and pious men would participate in the festivities by throwing flaming torches in the air and dancing. Levites standing on the steps between the men's and women's courtyards played music on lyres, harps, cymbals, and trumpets. "He who has not seen the joy of the water-drawing celebration has never seen joy in his life," says the Talmud.

The Sukkah

Beginning with Ezra the Scribe (fifth century B.C.E.), the sukkah became central to the holiday. The sukkah, or booth, can refer to the temporary dwellings or tents of the ancient Israelites who wandered in the desert, or later to harvesters' huts. The sukkah probably resembled the latter more closely with its thatched roof and greenery.

After the destruction of the Second Temple (70 C.E.) and the dispersion of the Jewish people, the emphasis shifted from Sukkot's mostly agricultural origins to Sukkot as a historical holiday, commemorating the period when the Israelites wandered in the desert for forty years under God's protection and shelter on their way to the promised land. Still, the memory of Sukkot as a joyous harvest holiday was never far from mind.

Requirements for the Sukkah

A sukkah resembles a makeshift hut, and can be constructed of any material. The frame can be of metal or plastic piping, or wood. The walls are most commonly covered with tarpaulin, burlap, canvas, and wood. The walls should be no more than ten yards high and only two walls and part of a third are required. The fourth can be an adjoining part of the house or left open

Left: Decorating the sukkah can be a delightful and creative project involving the entire family. Below: This sukkah decoration was made by an Italian Jew, Israel David Luzzato, around 1833. It also contains a biblical quotation from Lev. 23:42.

entirely. The *skhakh*, or roof covering, should be of something that grows and has been cut: evergreen branches, leafy branches, or bamboo poles are all acceptable. The *skhakh* should be thick enough to afford shade, but sparse enough so that stars can be seen at night. The sukkah should be sturdy enough so that it does not easily collapse, but not so strong that it can withstand gale-force winds. It is an exquisite balance between exposure and shelter, precariousness and protection.

Living in the Sukkah

In the Book of Leviticus, the Israelites are commanded to dwell in booths for seven days. In the Talmud, the Rabbis say that the sukkah should be the permanent dwelling for the week, and the home the temporary one—but this is more easily accomplished in a warm climate than in a cold one. Since the main feature of the holiday is joy, and since it also says in the Bible in reference to Sukkot "You shall have nothing but joy" (Deut. 16:15), the Rabbis were extremely careful to make certain that no discomfort was attached to observing this commandment. For instance, Jews are not required to eat in the sukkah in the rain. Although some people study and even sleep in the sukkah, most people just enjoy the sukkah by partaking of as many meals as possible in it, weather permitting.

WINGS
Lamed Shapiro

Author of short stories and translator of English classics into Yiddish; while most of his original writings deal with Jewish life of the past, his meticulous style was completely modern (1878–1948).

My father never built a *sukkah* for Sukkot; nevertheless, we still had a sukkah for the sacred festival. What's more, it was a beautiful one. All year long it was simply a plain pantry room, where one could find a sack of potatoes, a string of onions, a barrel of borscht, and other edibles. It bore not even the slightest trace of holiness, and no one ever dreamt that it served as a sukkah. If anyone had looked up to the ceiling, he would have seen a clever device that could convert the pantry to a sukkah: the ceiling was made of bars and crates. But who would glance up to the ceiling in the middle of the year? Therefore, everyone thought it was simply a pantry.

Still, each year on the day before Sukkot, the room became a *sukkah*. My older brother climbed up on the roof, fussed with something, and suddenly two big black wings opened up above the pantry. The bars were immediately covered with green boughs and thatching, the potatoes and onions vanished, a white cloth was draped over the borscht barrel, and a table, chair, and couch appeared. My father faithfully fulfilled the precept of residing in the *sukkah*—eating, drinking, and sleeping there. The entire house, usually higher than the pantry, was now lower than it. The pantry now proudly spread its wings over the house as though to say, "I'm a sukkah," seemingly ready to fly to the blue sky and bright sun.

From *The Jewish Government and Other Stories*. Originally published in 1971 by T. Wayne Publishers, New York.

HASUKKAH MAH YAFFAH*
Text by Harry Coopersmith

Folk Song

Ha - su - ka   ma ya - fa, u - ma tov la-
she - vet ba.   - she - vet ba. La la la la la   la la la
u - ma tov la - she - vet ba.   la - she - vet ba.

Ha-suka   ma na'a   u-ma tov le-e-chol ba.
La-la-la—·

No-de lo, no-de lo   ki l'o-lam chas-do.
La-la-la—·

How lovely is the Sukkah!
To enter it is a delight.
Welcome! How nice it is
to eat in it. Let's thank our
God for he is always gracious.

From *More of the Songs We Sing*. © 1971 The United Synagogue of America. Used with permission.

*See music on page 116.

"On the first day, you shall take for yourselves the product of goodly trees, branches of palm trees, boughs of leafy trees, and willows of the brook" (Lev. 23:40).

The sukkah is a place of hospitality and openness. It is traditional to invite a forebear each night as a symbolic guest, which is a kabbalistic or mystical influence. The ushpizin, or guests, are: Abraham, Isaac, Jacob, Joseph, Moses, Aaron, and David. There are those who even set up a chair in the sukkah in the "guest's" honor. Today, some Jews invite women matriarchs as well: Sarah, Rebekah, Rachel, Leah, Miriam, Deborah, and Hannah. Inviting guests, especially those in need, or those who do not have a sukkah of their own, reflects the spirit of the festival.

The Four Species

Another ritual closely associated with Sukkot is the *Arba'ah Minim*, or four species. The Book of Leviticus says, "On the first day, you shall take for yourselves the product of goodly trees, branches of palm trees, boughs of leafy trees, and willows of the brook" (Lev. 23:40). The Rabbis interpreted the "product of goodly trees" as meaning the etrog, or citron; the "branches of palm trees" as the palm branches; the "boughs of leafy trees" as the myrtle; and "willows of the brook" as willows. The palm branch bound with three myrtles to the right and two willows to the left constitutes the lulav. The Talmudic Rabbis interpreted "You shall take for yourselves" in the above verse as implying ownership. All people should therefore own their own set of the lulav and etrog and are encouraged to buy particularly beautiful specimens of the four species, especially the etrog.

The lulav is shaken before (when saying the blessing) and during the *Hallel* (songs of praise from the Book of Psalms), but never on Shabbat. Later in the service, the lulav and etrog are carried in a procession around the synagogue while chanting *hoshanot*—hymns ending with the refrain *hosha-na*—O help us. The *hoshana* circuit is performed once a day until Hoshana Rabbah (see below).

The Significance of the Four Species and Sukkah

Interpretations abound as to the significance of the four species. According to a midrash (a homiletical interpretation of Scripture), the etrog was the fruit given to Adam by Eve. Another interpretation is that we serve God with all our body—the etrog being the heart, the myrtle being the eye, the willow being the mouth, and the palm being the spine. Similarly, the commandment of sitting in the sukkah is one that entails one's whole being.

The significance of the sukkah also has many explanations and theories. For some, the sukkah symbolizes the ephemeral quality of life. For others, it is reminiscent of the upheavals and uprootedness of the Jewish people who have wandered all over the world, just as the ancient Israelites wandered in the desert. For still others, it tells of a fragile time in Jewish history, when the children of Israel were in the process of being formed into a people in the desert, and were in a suspended state between slavery and freedom, between the dream and its fulfillment.

Some see the sukkah as sensitizing those who are well-off to those who are less fortunate. The sukkah demonstrates that security does not have to lie within the four walls of an expensive house, and that worthwhile achievements cannot be defined or measured solely by the acquisition of material possessions. Other goals lie ahead; no one has arrived at his or her final destination. The sukkah becomes but a stop on the way, a temporary place to hang one's hat before resuming the journey.

Although rickety, the sukkah affords a spiritual, if not a physical, shelter. It makes one contemplate on a deeper level what is permanent and what is temporary, what protects and what leaves one vulnerable, what makes a home and what does not. There is an open quality to the sukkah, since it requires only three walls and a roof that is open to the stars. For many Jews, that is a reminder to have an open heart and a generous spirit—to be open to God, nature, and humanity.

Hoshana Rabbah

Hoshana Rabbah, the seventh day of Sukkot, is characterized by seven processions (or encirclements), instead of one, around the synagogue. It is called Hoshana Rabbah, or the "Great Hoshana,"

HOW TO BLESS AND WAVE THE LULAV

Hold the lulav upright in the right hand, with the three myrtles to the right and the two willows to the left. Pick the etrog up in the left hand with the tip (pittum) up and the stem facing down. Turn the etrog upside down. Bring your hands together. Recite the following blessing: *Barukh Atah Adonai Eloheinu melekh haolam asher kideshanu b'mitzvotav v'tzivanu al netilat lulav.* (Blessed are You, O Lord our God, king of the universe, who has sanctified us through His commandments and commanded us to take the palm branch.)

On the first day of Sukkot, recite the *shehehe'yanu blessing*—*Barukh Atah Adonai Eloheinu melekh haolam shehehe'yanu v'kiymanu v'higiyanu laz'man hazeh.* (Blessed are You, O Lord our God, king of the universe, who has given us life, sustained us, and enabled us to reach this moment.)

Turn the etrog right-side up (tip up, stem down), and shake the species in six directions. The motion is to stretch out your arm and bring it in. Shake the lulav three times in each direction in the following order—in front; to the right; over the shoulder; to the left; upward; and downward. (The lulav pointed up is lowered, never pointed down). All the while, keep your hands together, so the four species are never separated.

SHLOMIT BONAH SUKKAT SHALOM*

Shlo - mit bo - na - su - ka mu - e - ret - v'y - ru -
- ka al kein hi a - su - ka ha - yom v' -
- ein zo stam su - ka mu - e - ret v'y - ru - ka Shlo -
- mit bo - na su - kat sha - lom

Shlomit is building a sukkah
A bright and green sukkah
That's why she's so busy
But it's no ordinary sukkah
Shlomit is building a sukkah of peace!

Music and lyrics by Naomi Shemer
© by the author, ACUM, Israel.

*See music on page 116.

Creative sukkah decoration in Los Angeles.

for the many *hoshanot* recited and the circuits completed. The seven circuits are symbolic of the seven circuits made by the priests around the Temple's altar. Willow branches that have taken on the name of *hoshanot* are beaten, symbolizing to some the casting away of sins. According to the Zohar, the chief kabbalistic work, the willows are beaten to awaken the force that sends the water upon which the willows depend. They are later destroyed once the day of judgment is complete. This conforms to an ancient belief that the world is judged on Hoshana Rabbah, the last day of Sukkot, for the water it will receive and upon which it relies.

There is a tradition to view Hoshana Rabbah as a mini–Yom Kippur, when the final seal is given to the verdict rendered on Yom Kippur. It is a way to lengthen the period of penitence and postpone the day of final judgment, giving a last chance to those who did not make full use of Yom Kippur's grace. Melodies of the High Holy Days, particularly Yom Kippur, are often chanted, and the cantor may wear a white *kittel*, as on the High Holy Days. There is a tradition that is not widely known or observed, of staying up all night to study on the eve of Hoshana Rabbah.

- It has become a custom to build a communal sukkah adjacent to the synagogue for those who have no sukkah.
- Although the biblical injunction to "dwell in booths" is for seven days, it is particularly important to sit and eat in the sukkah on the first night or at least, even if it rains, to make kiddush and break bread there. The blessing in the sukkah is: *Barukh Atah Adonai Eloheinu melekh haolam asher kideshanu b'mitzvotav v'tzivanu leshev basukkah.* (Blessed are You, O Lord our God, king of the universe, who has sanctified us with His commandments and enjoined us to dwell in the sukkah.) This blessing is followed on the first night by the shehehe'yanu blessing: *Barukh Atah Adonai Eloheinu melekh haolam shehehe'yanu v'kiymanu v'higiyanu laz'man hazeh.* (Blessed are You, O Lord our God, king of the universe, who has given us life, sustained us, and enabled us to reach this moment.) On the second night the order of the blessings is reversed.
- Acquiring the finest specimens of the *arba'ah minim* (lulav and etrog) as *hiddur mitzvah* (enhancement of the commandment). An etrog should be yellow, firm, rough in texture, unblemished, and beautifully formed with the pittum (tip) intact; the lulav should be green and straight, the top unbroken, and the leaves of the willow and myrtle should be fresh and unwilted.
- Inviting our ancestors, known as the *ushpizin*, into the sukkah. A poster with their names can be hung in the sukkah.
- Decorating the sukkah elaborately and creatively. Hanging fruit, vegetables, gourds, and Indian corn from the "roof"; Rosh Hashanah cards, posters, pictures, crafts, crepe paper, paper chains, and strung cranberries, peanuts, and popcorn can adorn the walls. Imagination is the key to creative sukkah decorating, using the holiday themes of Sukkot as a harvest festival, a pilgrimage festival, and a time of joy.
- Reading of the Book of Kohelet (Ecclesiastes) in the synagogue on the Shabbat of Sukkot. The relationship of this megillah to Sukkot is not obvious. The book opens with the words "Vanity of vanity, all is vanity" and is a jaded description of life, seemingly unrelated to the joyousness of the holiday. However, Kohelet suggests a balance to one's life—"there is a time for everything—a time for weeping and a time for laughing." Sukkot is the time to rejoice after the solemnity of the High Holy Days. Kohelet also suggests that the most important things in life are the basic simple pleasures—eat, drink, and enjoy oneself—which is not hard to relate to Sukkot.
- Collecting several etrogim to make jam or marmalade after the holiday.

Hiddur Mitzvah
(Enhancing the Holiday)

The concept of *hiddur mitzvah* (literally "beautifying the commandment") is most closely associated with Sukkot, when one was encouraged to acquire beautiful specimens of the four species. A lovely etrog container made of metal, wood, or other material is another way to make the holiday more special.

Acquiring excellent specimens of seasonal fruits and vegetables with which to decorate the sukkah can likewise embellish the holiday. Some people hang plastic fruit and vegetables so they can be used year after year. House plants can be brought into the sukkah for an extra touch of greenery. Beautiful artwork made by children in the family can be laminated and hung in the sukkah and used from one year to another.

A season is set for everything, a time for every experience under heaven.
A time for being born and a time for dying,
A time for planting and a time for uprooting the planted;
A time for slaying and a time for healing,
A time for tearing down and a time for building up;
A time for weeping and a time for laughing,
A time for wailing and a time for dancing;
A time for throwing stones and a time for gathering stones,
A time for embracing and a time for shunning embraces;
A time for seeking and a time for losing,
A time for keeping and a time for discarding;
A time for ripping and a time for sewing,
A time for silence and a time for speaking;
A time for loving and a time for hating;
A time for war and a time for peace.

From Ecclesiastes, Ch. 3. From *TANACH: A New Translation of the Holy Scriptures*, © 1985 by the Jewish Publication Society.

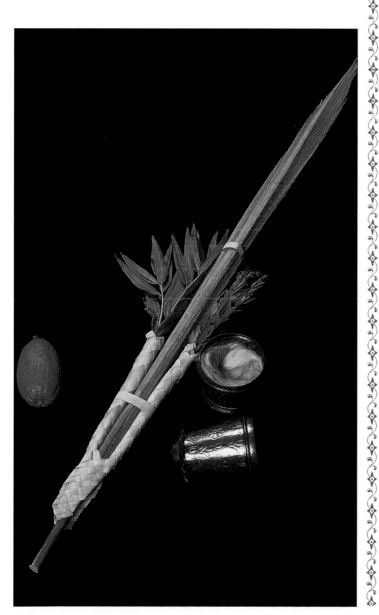

Left: This beautiful lulav is straight and erect with three myrtle branches to the right and two willow branches to the left. The citron or etrog is yellow and rough in texture and unblemished. A lovely metal etrog container safeguards the etrog when not in use. Right: A 1947 photo of Jewish children in Palestine (some of them refugees) reciting the blessing over the lulav in celebration of the ancient festival of Sukkot.

SHEMINI ATZERET AND SIMHAT TORAH

Shemini Atzeret, known as the Eighth Day of Assembly, is based upon the verse in the Book of Numbers (29:35), "On the eighth day you should hold a solemn gathering. You shall not work at your occupations." The Rabbis did not consider Shemini Atzeret the end of Sukkot, but a holiday unto itself. The sukkah is no longer used; neither is the lulav or etrog. The Rabbis believed that God, in His reluctance to leave His people, ordained an additional holiday. In the Diaspora, Simhat Torah is considered the second day of Shemini Atzeret, while in Israel both holidays are combined into one.

Because the critical rainy season begins at this time of year in Israel, the water or rain motif has been important. It peaks on Shemini Atzeret when a prayer for rain is recited. This prayer is particular to Shemini Atzeret and not recited on Sukkot, because rain is not desired in the sukkah. The statement "You cause the wind to blow and rain to fall" is added to the *Amidah* prayer (the principal prayer said at every service while standing) and is said in every *Amidah* from Shemini Atzeret until Passover. The prayer for life-giving rain reminds Jews in the Diaspora of their ties to the land of Israel, which is so dependent on rain for sustenance and survival. At the same time, Jews are also mindful that rain can be a blessing and a curse, and that a flood can be as disastrous as a drought.

Rejoicing in the Torah

The second day of Shemini Atzeret is known as Simhat Torah, "Rejoicing in the Torah," a holiday first mentioned in the eleventh century. On Simhat Torah, Jews do not celebrate a historical event, but a cyclical event—the completion of the Torah reading—and it is a joyous day, indeed. In fact, the happiness of Sukkot is only surpassed by the frenzied merriment of Simhat Torah. On the eve of Simhat Torah bedlam reigns in the synagogue. There is an air of jubilation mingled with expectation. Children crowd the synagogue waving flags and often carrying apples and candles. There are seven *hakafot*, or encirclements, with men and women carrying the Torahs, all of which have been removed from the ark. The processions are accompanied by exuberant singing and dancing. In some synagogues, this is followed by three *aliyot* from the last chapter of Deuteronomy. Simhat Torah is the only holiday when the Torah is read at night.

In the morning of Simhat Torah, there is again much festivity, fun, and frivolity. Everyone is called to the Torah and given

GESHEM

Prayer for rain recited on Shemini Atzeret

Remember Abraham, his heart poured out to You like water.
You blessed him, as a tree planted near water;
You saved him when he went through fire and water.

For Abraham's sake, do not withhold water.

Remember Isaac, his birth foretold while angels drank cool water.
At Moriah his blood was almost spilled like water;
In the desert he dug deep to find springs of water.

For Isaac's sake, grant the gift of water.

Remember Jacob, who with his staff forded Jordan's water.
Gallantly he showed his love beside a well of water;
He struggled, victoriously, with a creature of fire and water.

For Jacob's sake, do not withhold water.

Remember Moses, whose basket rocked in reeds and water.
In Midian he gave his sheep ample grass and water;
He struck the rock, and then the tribes drank sweet water.

For Moses' sake, grant the gift of water.

Remember Aaron the priest and his ritual immersions in water.
On Yom Kippur he kept the rites with water;
He read from the Torah and bathed himself in water.

For Aaron's sake, do not withhold water.

Remember Israel's tribes; You brought them through water.
For their sake brackish marsh became sweet water;
Their descendants' blood was spilled for You like water.

For the people Israel's sake, grant the gift of water.

Reprinted from *Siddur Sim Shalom*, edited by Rabbi Jules Harlow. © 1985 by the Rabbinical Assembly. Reprinted by permission of the Rabbinical Assembly.

Rainfall is essential to Israel during the winter months, because water is so scarce. This photo shows the Sea of Galilee (Lake Kinneret), Israel's only freshwater lake, with the city of Tiberias in the background.

an honor called an *aliyah*. The honor of an *aliyah* when the final verses of the Torah are read is given to a worthy congregant, known as the *Hatan Torah* (groom of the Torah). This is immediately followed by the honor known as *Hatan Bereshit* (groom of Genesis), given to another deserving individual, followed by the reading of the opening verses of the Torah.

Thus, the reading of the Torah never ends: the final verses of Deuteronomy are always followed by the opening verses of Genesis, emphasizing that the teaching, study, and practice of Torah are continuous and continuing processes. A nineteenth-century Hasidic rabbi, the Gerer rebbe once commented that the rejoicing on Simhat Torah does not come from concluding the Torah, as is commonly thought, but from beginning the Torah all over again.

In one of the final *aliyot*, called *Kol Hane'arim*, all children younger than bar and bat mitzvah age are called to the Torah, and a *tallit*, or prayer shawl, is held over their heads like a canopy.

Melodies from other holidays are often interjected into the *Musaf* (additional) service, underscoring the playfulness of the holiday—the perfect foil for the solemn dignity of the High Holy Days. Simhat Torah affirms that Jews take the Torah seriously, but not gloomily. Indeed, Simhat Torah illustrates that for Jews the Torah does not restrict but liberates. It is not a burden, but a joy. The relationship between the Jewish people and the Torah is warm and loving, familiar and familial. On Simhat Torah, the Torah is feted much like a bride at her wedding, with song, dance, and merriment.

B'SIMCHAT TORAH*

Si-su v' - sim - chu   b' -sim-chat to - ra   u - t'nu ka - vod la - to - ra   si - su v'- sim - chu   b'-sim-chat to - ra   u - t'nu ka - vod la - to - ra   si -su v' - sim - chu   b' -sim-chat to - ra   u - t'nu ka - vod   la - to - ra

si - su v' - sim-chu   si - su v' - sim - chu   si - su v'- sim - chu b' - sim-chat to - ra   si - su v' - sim - chu b'-sim-chat to - ra   u - t'nu ka - vod la - to - ra   si - su v'-sim - chu b'- sim-chat to - ra   u - t'nu ka - vod la - to - ra

Let us rejoice on Simchat Torah
and honor the Torah.

Lyrics: Traditional. Music: Y. Paikov.
© by the author, ACUM, Israel.

*See music on page 117.

A joyous and spirited Simhat Torah celebration in Jerusalem.

Sukkot is the time for hearty meals and hospitality.

SUKKOT MENU

The sukkot menu reflects the harvest bounty. Traditional dishes include stuffed foods (symbolizing opulence) and strudel.

Stuffed Cabbage
White Bean Soup
Assorted Peppers Salad
Lemon Chicken
Steamed Sesame Broccoli
Vegetable Rice Pilaf
Hazelnut Cookies
Plum Strudel
Fruit Platter: Pomegranates, Pears, Apples, Bananas,
Dried Fruit, Assorted Nuts

Stuffed Cabbage

Stuffed cabbage is traditional on Sukkot and well worth the effort. It is best served a day or two after it is made, so that it can marinate.

Sauce
- 2 tablespoons vegetable oil
- 1 large onion, chopped
- ⅓ cup brown or white sugar
- 1 can (16 ounces) diced tomatoes, undrained
- 2 cans (8 ounces each) tomato sauce
- Juice of 1 large lemon
- ½ cup raisins

In a large pot, heat oil and sauté onion until translucent. Add sugar and stir until dissolved. Add tomatoes with juice. Add tomato sauce, lemon juice, and raisins. Bring to a boil. Cover and simmer while preparing filling for cabbage rolls.

Filling
- 1 large head green cabbage
- 1 to 1¼ pounds lean ground shoulder steak
- 1 egg, lightly beaten
- 3 to 4 tablespoons uncooked rice
- 1 tablespoon minced onion
- 2 tablespoons chili sauce (optional)
- 4 tablespoons water
- 1 teaspoon salt
- ¼ teaspoon pepper

Remove core of cabbage. Gently separate leaves. Shred remaining cabbage and add to sauce if desired. Blanch leaves in boiling water for 5 minutes. Drain. Place leaves in a large pot and cover with water. Bring to a boil.

To make filling, combine all remaining ingredients and blend well. To assemble, place a heaping tablespoon of filling in the center of each leaf, fold sides to cover meat, and roll. Secure with a toothpick.

Gently add stuffed cabbage to cooked sauce and continue to simmer for 1½ hours. Remove toothpicks before serving.

Makes approximately 14 to 16 pieces of stuffed cabbage.

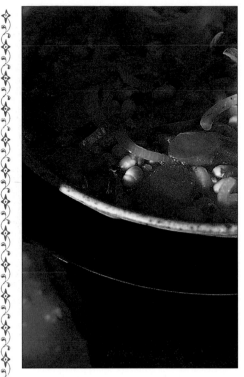

White Bean Soup.

White Bean Soup

This very easy but wonderful soup has a delicate flavor that is enhanced by herbs. Use fresh herbs when available.

- 2 cans (16 ounces each) cannellini (white kidney) beans, undrained
- 4 cups water, chicken stock, or vegetable broth
- 2 medium onions, sliced
- 1 cup carrots, sliced
- 2 stalks celery, chopped
- 2 bay leaves
- ½ teaspoon thyme
- ½ teaspoon marjoram
- ½ teaspoon sage
- 4 sprigs fresh parsley
- 4 sprigs fresh dill
- ¼ teaspoon pepper

Combine ingredients in a medium saucepan. Simmer 30 minutes or until vegetables are tender. Serve hot.

Serves 8.

Stuffed Cabbage.

Assorted Peppers Salad.

Assorted Peppers Salad

When peppers are roasted, it makes for a more tender salad, but I like the crunch of uncooked peppers.

- 2 large green bell peppers
- 2 large red peppers
- 2 large yellow peppers
- 1 large purple pepper
- 1 large orange pepper

Core and remove seeds from each pepper. Slice peppers lengthwise into thin strips.

Note: If you prefer to soften the peppers, place halved peppers on a cookie sheet and broil for about 15 minutes or until blistered. Turn occasionally. Enclose in paper or plastic bag to steam for about 10 minutes while cooling. Peel, then slice.

Marinade
- 3 tablespoons lemon juice
- 3 tablespoons lime juice
- 6 tablespoons olive oil
- ½ teaspoon salt
- ½ teaspoon pepper
- 2 garlic cloves, finely minced
- 2 teaspoons fresh parsley (½ teaspoon dry)
- 1 teaspoon Italian seasoning
- ½ teaspoon oregano or basil

In a jar, combine all ingredients. Shake well. Pour over peppers and refrigerate 3 to 4 hours.

Serves 8.

Lemon Chicken

Concentrated frozen lemonade is the secret ingredient in this luscious chicken recipe.

- 1 egg, lightly beaten
- ½ 6-ounce can frozen lemonade, thawed
- 2 tablespoons soy sauce
- ½ cup fine dry bread crumbs
- 3 tablespoons sesame seeds
- 1 teaspoon thyme
- 1 teaspoon lemon peel
- 1 teaspoon salt
- ¾ teaspoon grated ginger
- 8 skinless, boneless chicken breast halves
- 3 tablespoons vegetable oil
- 1 tablespoon pareve margarine

Preheat oven to 350 degrees F.

Combine egg, lemonade concentrate, and soy sauce in a bowl. In second bowl, mix together bread crumbs, sesame seeds, thyme, lemon peel, salt, and ginger. Dip chicken in lemonade mixture, then roll in bread crumb mixture. In a large skillet, heat oil and margarine. Sauté chicken on each side, until lightly brown, approximately 3 to 5 minutes per side. Remove and place in a baking dish.

Lemon Sauce
- 2 tablespoons cornstarch
- 1 cup water
- Remaining 3 ounces thawed lemonade
- Lemon juice
- 4 teaspoons soy sauce
- 2 tablespoons sugar
- Lemon slices to garnish

Dissolve cornstarch in water and set aside. Add enough lemon juice to the lemonade to make ½ cup of liquid. In a small saucepan, place lemonade liquid, soy sauce, sugar, and cornstarch mixture. Bring to a boil. Stir until thick. Pour over chicken.

Place chicken in oven and bake 15 to 20 minutes. Garnish with lemon slices.

Serves 8.

Steamed Sesame Broccoli

- 1½ heads broccoli (about 2½ pounds)
- 2 tablespoons olive oil
- 2 teaspoons minced garlic
- Juice of 1 lemon
- ½ teaspoon salt
- 1 tablespoon sesame seeds, toasted

Cut broccoli into florets. Steam for 3 to 5 minutes. Place olive oil in skillet or wok and sauté garlic. Add broccoli and remaining ingredients. Toss together and sauté 2 to 3 more minutes.

Serves 8.

Lemon Chicken and Steamed Sesame Broccoli.

Plum Strudel.

Plum Strudel

With their tart-sweet taste, plums make a lovely Sukkot strudel.

- 6 large phyllo sheets, unfolded, at room temperature
- Melted pareve margarine (about ¾ stick)
- Sugar for sprinkling

Defrost phyllo dough according to package instructions. Phyllo dries out easily, so do not remove sheets until filling ingredients are assembled. Remove just the sheets you need for recipe and keep them covered with plastic wrap and damp cloth. Cover remaining sheets well with plastic wrap, replace in box, and refrigerate or refreeze.

Filling
- 8 to 10 firm, ripe medium plums, pitted and sliced
- ¼ cup sugar, part brown
- ½ teaspoon ground nutmeg
- ⅛ teaspoon allspice
- 1 teaspoon lemon rind
- ½ cup finely chopped nuts (pecans, walnuts, or almonds)
- ¼ cup bread crumbs

Preheat oven to 375 degrees F.

Combine plums, sugar, nutmeg, allspice, and lemon rind; toss well. Spread one phyllo sheet on parchment paper or waxed paper and brush lightly with margarine. Repeat with another phyllo sheet. Spread with 2 tablespoons of chopped nuts. Repeat process with another 2 buttered sheets and 2 more tablespoons of nuts. Top with 2 buttered sheets. Sprinkle with ¼ cup nuts and ¼ cup bread crumbs.

Place filling in a long strip, 2 inches from edge, and leave a 1-inch margin on each of the shorter sides. Fold in shorter edges and gently roll up dough.

Place rolled strudel seam-side down on greased cookie sheet and brush with margarine and sprinkle with sugar. Bake for 35 to 45 minutes or until golden brown. Let cool and serve warm.

Makes 1 large strudel.

Vegetable Rice Pilaf

Different kinds of rice have unique qualities and flavors. I particularly like jasmine and basmati. For this recipe, use a little less than 3 cups of water for basmati rice, and use 3 cups of water with regular long grain rice.

- 2 tablespoons olive oil
- 1 medium onion, finely chopped
- 6 ounces fresh mushrooms, sliced
- 1 stalk celery, finely chopped
- ½ green pepper, finely chopped
- 1½ cups long grain or rinsed basmati rice
- 3 cups water, vegetable stock, or chicken broth
- Salt and pepper to taste
- Dried basil to garnish

Heat oil and sauté onions until translucent. Add mushrooms, celery, and green pepper and sauté about 2 minutes. Add rice and sauté. Add broth and salt and pepper to taste. Bring to a boil. Reduce heat, cover, and simmer 17 minutes. Garnish with dried basil if desired. For softer rice, use more water.

Serves 8.

Hazelnut Cookies

Hazelnuts, or filberts, are more commonly used in European baking, but are gaining in popularity in the United States.

- ¾ cup pareve unsalted margarine
- ¾ cup sugar
- 1 egg
- 1 teaspoon vanilla or hazelnut liqueur (Frangelico®)
- 2 cups flour
- ¼ teaspoon salt
- 1 cup lightly toasted hazelnuts, finely chopped

Preheat oven to 350 degrees F.

Cream margarine and sugar. Add egg and vanilla or liqueur. Blend in flour and salt and mix well. Add hazelnuts. Chill in refrigerator for 30 minutes. Form into 1-inch balls. Place balls on ungreased cookie sheets and flatten with fork. Bake for 15 to 18 minutes or until cookies are lightly colored.

Makes about 40 cookies.

Note: To toast hazelnuts, spread a single layer on a baking sheet and bake about 8 minutes at 350 degrees F or until nuts are lightly browned under skins. Cool, then chop, or chop first, then toast and cool.

CHAPTER FOUR

HANUKKAH

There are approximately two Hebrew months between the end of Sukkot and the beginning of Hanukkah. Scholars have noted that Hanukkah originally was celebrated as a second Sukkot ("Sukkot in the month of Kislev"). This link between Hanukkah and Sukkot is mentioned in the second book of Maccabees in the Apocrypha (books not canonized into the Hebrew Bible) abridged from a larger work written by a devout Hellenized Jew, Jason of Cyrene. *"Now it so happened that the cleansing of the sanctuary took place on the very day on which it was profaned by foreigners on the twenty-fifth of the same month, which is Kislev. And they celebrated it for eight days with gladness like a Feast of Tabernacles remembering how, not long before, during the Feast of Tabernacles they had been wandering like wild beasts in the mountains and the caves. So bearing wands wreathed with leaves and beautiful boughs and palms, they offered hymns of praise to Him who had prospered the cleansing of His own place. And they passed a public ordinance and decree that the whole Jewish nation should observe these days."* (Maccabees II, 10:5–8)

The year Hanukkah occurred, Jews had been unable to celebrate Sukkot. In fact, Sukkot may not have been observed

Opposite: A Hasidic family gathers around an oil-burning Hannukah menorah (hanukiyah) on the sixth night of the festival. Left: A nineteenth-century illustration showing the celebration of Hanukkah, with the lighting of Hanukkah lights and the playing of a game of chess.

properly for several years since the Temple had been defiled by the Syrians and the service halted. Solomon's Temple had been dedicated on Sukkot and this may have influenced the Maccabees who, after cleansing and purifying the Second Temple, ordered the celebration of an eight-day festival, which became known as Hanukkah.

This is how Hanukkah originally took on some aspects of Sukkot. Other aspects included the carrying of the lulav, the recitation of the *Hallel*, the joyousness of Sukkot, and its eight-day length (which included Shemini Atzeret). Except for the lulav, these features of Sukkot have remained part of Hanukkah.

HISTORY OF HANUKKAH

Hanukkah is the first nonbiblical holiday to be incorporated into the Jewish calendar, and harks back to a real set of historical events and circumstances. To understand the origins of Hanukkah, we must go back to the fourth century B.C.E., when Alexander the Great conquered the Persian empire, including Palestine.

The Jews fared well under Alexander the Great, as they had under the Persians. Alexander allowed them to live according to their ancestral laws (which he also accorded other peoples). Unfortunately, his reign was short-lived, lasting but a decade. Hellenism as a force continued to grow, and grew considerably after Alexander died. The most cosmopolitan and sophisticated civilization the world had ever known, a blend of Greek and Eastern traditions, Hellenism spread rapidly as various nationalities and peoples adopted Greek manners, mode of dress, speech, values, philosophy, art, and culture. Even Jews in Palestine felt the Hellenistic influence, and many were attracted to it, particularly Judea's upper class, some of whom had their children educated in the best Greek schools and academies.

After Alexander's death, his empire was divided. Palestine, strategically located as a bridge between Africa and Asia, was caught between the Ptolemies, the rulers of Egypt, to the south, and the Seleucids, the rulers of Syria, to the north. For about a hundred years, Palestine fell under the Ptolemaic kingdom. Eventually, the Seleucids overtook Palestine, and that is when the story of Hanukkah officially begins.

Under the Seleucids, Hellenism became government policy and a test of loyalty to the king. Some of the wealthiest and most accomplished of the Jewish upper classes were attracted to Hellenism and were pro-Syria. The lower classes, the less educated, and the conservatives were pro-Egypt.

Antiochus IV Epiphanes assumed the Graeco-Syrian throne around 175 B.C.E. By most accounts, he was capricious, unstable, and perhaps mad. Externally, he waged war against Egypt, while internally he tried to mold the different peoples of his kingdom into a monolithic empire, with Hellenism as his tool.

Under the influence and wealth of a prominent Judean family, the Tobiads, Antiochus tried to get the Jews to assimilate. He deposed their High Priest, Onias III, replacing him with his brother, Joshua, a Hellenized Jew who had changed his Hebrew name to the Greek name of Jason. Jason wanted to turn Jerusalem into a polis, or Greek city-state, to be called Antioch-

The Battle of the Maccabees. Mattathias and his five sons, especially the middle son, Judah, led the revolt against the Graeco-Syrians and their king, Antiochus IV, and his cruel policy of forcibly Hellenizing Judea.

at-Jerusalem. He constructed a gymnasium and encouraged Greek sports. Eventually, Jason was replaced with a more extreme Hellenist, the High Priest Menelaus, a leader of the pro-Syrian party. For the first time in Jewish history, a king, rather than heredity, determined the High Priesthood.

After Antiochus was defeated by Rome and deprived of Egypt, he plundered the Temple in Jerusalem and tried to forcibly Hellenize Judea. He issued a decree that all people were to serve pagan gods and introduced Syrian cults into the Temple. There was a grass-roots revolt, and Antiochus forbade the study of Torah, the observance of the Sabbath and dietary laws, the rite of circumcision, and all other precepts of Judaism. Anyone caught observing any Jewish practice was sentenced to death. Thousands of Jews died (becoming history's first religious martyrs) defying Antiochus' orders.

In 167 B.C.E., a statue of Zeus Olympius was erected in the Temple in Jerusalem, which was defiled and turned into a Grecian shrine. Sacrifices of pigs were instituted there and in shrines in provincial towns throughout Judea.

The Revolt

When Antiochus' representatives came to the small town of Modiin, near Lydda, they set up an altar to force Jews to submit to the decrees by sacrificing a pig. A Jewish Hellenist who complied was slain by the aged priest, Mattathias, of the Hasmonean family, who could bear no more. Mattathias, though a traditionalist, was no pacifist. "Let everyone who is zealous for the law and that would maintain the covenant come forth after me," he proclaimed. With his five sons, John (Yohanan), Simon, Judah, Eliezer, and Jonathan he attracted a band of guerilla fighters. They fled into the mountains and launched successful guerilla warfare against the Syrians, thanks largely to the leadership and bravery of the middle son, Judah Maccabee, a brilliant strategist. As a result of his knowing the terrain well, Judah was able to win significant victories against the Syrians through ambush and night attacks.

More than a war against Antiochus and his cruelties, it had become a civil war between assimilationist Jews and religious, faithful Jews. Joining Mattathias and his sons (known as the Maccabees) were the Hasidim (or Pietists, an ultratraditionalist religious sect, staunch defenders and upholders of the Jewish faith) as well as moderate Hellenists who formed a coalition that helped defeat the Syrians and liberate Jerusalem. After Judah defeated the Syrian general, Lysias, at Beth Zur, Lysias left the country and called off the persecution. With Lysias gone, Judah decided to march on Jerusalem. On the twenty-fifth of Kislev, 164 B.C.E. (by most accounts), Judah took Jerusalem and cleansed the Temple—three years after the Temple's desecration. The Temple was purified—the defiled altar was removed and a new one erected, new holy vessels were made, the menorah was relit, and the Temple was rededicated. That is why the holiday is called Hanukkah, meaning "dedication."

LYSIAS, THE GREEK GENERAL

Between 175 and 172 B.C.E., a people's revolt against the Hellenizers in Jerusalem erupted, threatening the very fabric of life in Judea. The Syrian king, Antiochus IV, fearing a complete breakdown of allegiance, as well as the spread of other such revolts throughout his empire, came to Jerusalem and savagely put the revolt down.

As soon as Antiochus left, however, the civil war between the Jewish traditionalists and the Hellenizers erupted once again. By this time, Judah Maccabee was in charge of a well-trained Jewish army and defeated a series of Syrian generals including Apollonius and Seron.

Antiochus decided that only the great General Lysias would be capable of defeating Judah and quashing the rebellion once and for all. Twice, however, Judah was able to defeat Lysias' forces. So Lysias decided to head his own army and confront the wily and brilliant strategist Judah Maccabee.

Lysias developed a new plan of attack; he decided to come to Jerusalem from the south and surprise Judah's guerilla forces. Anticipating Lysias' plan, Judah defeated him and then came to Jerusalem, where in 164 B.C.E. he recaptured and rededicated the Temple.

Unrest still rumbled throughout the countryside. Judah began to cleanse the country of Syrians and their cult. Lysias returned to Antioch to create a new army for a final confrontation.

Two years passed. Antiochus IV died, and his young son, Antiochus V, became the new king. Real power, however, lay in the hands of Lysias, guardian of the new king, regent, and supreme ruler of the land.

Now was the time to put an end to the troubles in Judea. Lysias listened attentively to the Hellenizers from Jerusalem and brought a large army to Jerusalem—larger and more powerful than before. Judah was defeated this time, and Lysias laid siege to Jerusalem, which suffered from a lack of food and water.

What Lysias did not know was that someone else was about to challenge his power, someone whom Antiochus IV had appointed before he died. Unable to share power, Lysias knew that he would have to retreat from Judea to confront a new threat in Antioch.

A wise and realistic general and leader, Lysias recognized that a compromise was needed between himself and Judah. He also realized that he had been drawn into an unnecessary conflict by the Jewish Hellenizers.

The document prepared by Antiochus V, with the personal hand of Lysias, ratified for Judah Maccabee the right of the Jews to live according to their "ancestral laws." Thus, further bloodshed was averted and Lysias retreated to Antioch. In 162 B.C.E., the religious freedom that Judah Maccabee and the traditionalists had fought for became a reality not only in the eyes of the Jews who lived in Judea, but also in the eyes of the Greek empire. By knowing when to retreat, Lysias permitted the Hasmonean dynasty, which had already fought for and won religious autonomy, to begin its long road toward political independence as well.

PSALM 30

Recited by Sephardic Jews after kindling Hanukkah lights.

A Song of David
A Song for the Dedication of the Temple.

I extol You, O Lord. You raised me up.
You did not permit foes to rejoice over me.

Lord, I cried out and You healed me.
You saved me from the pit of death.

Sing to the Lord, you faithful,
Acclaiming His holiness

His anger lasts a moment;
His love is for a lifetime.

Tears may linger for a night,
but joy comes with the dawn.

While at ease I once thought:
nothing can shake my security.

Favor me and I am a mountain of strength.
Hide Your face, Lord, and I am terrified.

To You, Lord, would I call;
before the Lord would I plead.

What profit is there if I am silenced,
what benefit if I go to my grave?

Will the dust praise You?
Will it proclaim Your faithfulness?

Hear me, Lord. Be gracious, be my help.

You turned my mourning into dancing.
You changed my sackcloth into robes of joy

that I might sing Your praise unceasingly,
that I might thank You, Lord my God, forever.

From *TANACH: A New Translation of the Holy Scripture*, © 1985 by The Jewish Publication Society.

THE REASON FOR HANUKKAH

[The Talmud asks:] Why [do we celebrate] Hanukkah? Our Sages taught: The twenty-fifth day of [the Hebrew month of] Kislev marks the beginning of the eight days of Hanukkah. Lamentation and fasting are forbidden.

For when the Greeks entered the Temple, they desecrated all the oil in the Holy of Holies. Then, when the Hasmonean power grew strong and overcame them [the Greeks], the [Hasmoneans] searched [for pure oil to rekindle the lamp] and found none, except for one jar, which was found lying with the seal of the High Priest still intact. Its contents, however, were sufficient for only one day. A miracle occurred and the supply lasted eight days. The following year [the Sages] established and instituted a festival [in commemoration of the miracle] with the singing of the Hallel combined with thankfulness.

From the Talmud, Shabbat 21b. Translated by A.C. Fellner.

THE FESTIVAL OF HANUKKAH

The Maccabees themselves decreed an eight-day festival to be observed yearly, perhaps modeled after the pattern of the Greeks, who decreed holidays following great events. Shortly after the death of Antiochus IV, the Maccabees persuaded his successor, Antiochus V, to rescind the edicts against the Jewish religion, and to reestablish Jewish autonomy. This eventually led to the reestablishment of a new Jewish commonwealth under the Hasmoneans (the dynasty of the Maccabees), which lasted about a hundred years.

Most accounts of this period are found in the Books of Maccabees I and II in the Apocrypha. Allusions to this period can be found in the biblical Book of Daniel, and in a non-historical medieval document called the Scroll of Antiochus. Josephus, the first-century Roman Jewish historian, refers to the festival as the Feast of Lights because "the right to serve God came to the people unexpectedly, like a sudden light."

THE RABBIS AND HANUKKAH

There are a few passing references to Hanukkah and no mention at all of Hanukkah lights in the Mishnah (codification of oral law compiled by Rabbi Judah the Prince [see page 104]). In the Gemara (commentary on the Mishnah) the Rabbis ask, "What is Hanukkah?" suggesting a certain ambivalence to the holiday and a need to search for a deeper meaning for a holiday that had been based upon military success. For the first time, they set forth an explanation for the kindling of the Hanukkah lights for eight days. The Rabbis refer to the miracle of Hanukkah, explaining that purified oil was in short supply because all other oil had been defiled. Only one flask of purified oil was found, barely enough for one day's supply. Because of a miracle, the oil lasted eight days. Hence, according to the Rabbis, this is why we celebrate Hanukkah for eight days and kindle Hanukkah lights. Although the authenticity of this explanation was questioned in the Middle Ages, the story of the oil has appealed to the collective Jewish imagination to the point that it is virtually impossible to omit it from the Hanukkah story.

By emphasizing the miracle of the oil and downplaying the military and political aspects of the holiday, the Rabbis added a special spiritual dimension to Hanukkah. By sanctioning the ritual of the lighting of the candles, they hoped to ensure the survival of the holiday. "Not by might, not by power, but by My spirit," is a verse from the prophet Zechariah (4:6) that is read for the Sabbath of Hanukkah, and reflects the rabbinic posture.

Centuries later, Zionists rediscovered Hanukkah as a holiday of national liberation. They identified with the military victories of the few who were able to defeat a stronger, more numerous foe, and who, like them, had recreated a Jewish nation on its own soil.

Unquestionably, Hanukkah as a holiday has a fascinating history. However, there were times when Hanukkah faded into obscurity and was even unpopular, as during Mishnaic times (about 200 C.E.), when the Rabbis lived under Roman rule and to celebrate an uprising would have been unwise. Moreover, they might have wanted to distance themselves from the Hasmonean dynasty, which had deteriorated. Hanukkah became popular in the Middle Ages and even more so in the nineteenth century after emancipation, when Jews were granted citizenship and lived among their Christian neighbors.

According to a 1990 CJF National Jewish Population Study, between 75 and 80 percent of Jews kindle Hanukkah lights, making it the second most-observed (after the Passover Seder) Jewish home ritual. Without a doubt, Hanukkah's proximity to Christmas and its anti-assimilationist message has turned this minor Jewish holiday into a major Jewish celebration.

HANEROT HALLALU— THESE CANDLES

The following passage is recited or sung after the Hanukkah candle lighting:

"These candles we kindle to recall the miracle and wonders and the battles that You carried out for our ancestors in those days and at this season through Your holy priests. Throughout all eight days of Hanukkah, these lights are sacred; we may not use them except to look upon them to thank You and praise Your great name for Your miracles, Your wonders, and Your deliverance."

HOW TO KINDLE THE HANUKKAH LIGHTS

With the *hanukiyah* facing you, place a candle in the *shamash* holder and place the candle for the first night on the extreme right side. On the second night, add an additional candle to the left of the first one. On each night, add another candle to the left of the previous one until all eight candleholders are used. Light the *shamash* first, and use it to kindle the other candles. Light the newest candle for that evening first. Then light the remaining candles from left to right. A total of forty-four candles will be used in the course of the holiday. On Friday evening, light the Hanukkah candles before the Sabbath candles. At the Sabbath's end, it is generally agreed that the Hanukkah candles are lit after the *Havdalah* service at home, but before *Havdalah* in the synagogue.

Recite the following blessings before kindling the Hanukkah lights: *Barukh Atah Adonai Eloheinu melekh haolam asher kideshanu b'mitzvotav v'tzivanu l'hadlik ner shel Hanukkah.*

Blessed are You, O Lord our God, king of the universe, who has sanctified us with His commandments and commanded us to kindle the Hanukkah lights.

Barukh Atah Adonai Eloheinu melekh haolam she'asah nissim l'avoteinu bayamim hahem bazman hazeh.

Blessed are You, O Lord our God, king of the universe, who performed miracles for our ancestors in days gone by and at this season.

The *shehehe'yanu* blessing is added on the first night only: *Barukh Atah Adonai Eloheinu melekh haolam shehehe'yanu v'kiyemanu v'higiyanu laz'man hazeh.*

Blessed are You, Lord our God, king of the universe, who has kept us in life, sustained us, and brought us to this season.

After the Hanukkah lights are kindled, *Hanerot Hallalu* (These Candles), *Maoz Tzur* (Rock of Ages), and other Hanukkah songs are sung.

A young girl lights Hanukkah candles as her brother looks on. Often each family member lights his or her own hanukiyah.

Families come together to celebrate the first night of Hanukkah. Shown are different styles of hanukiyot.

THE VICTORY OF THE SPIRIT

Hanukkah, the Feast of the Maccabees, celebrates a victory—not a military victory only, but a victory also of the spirit over things material. Not a victory only over external enemies—the Greeks; but a victory also over more dangerous internal enemies. A victory of the many over the ease-loving, safety-playing, privileged, powerful few who in their pliancy would have betrayed the best interests of the people, a victory of democracy over aristocracy.

As part of the eternal worldwide struggle for the democracy, the struggle of the Maccabees is of eternal worldwide interest. It is a struggle of the Jews of today as well as those of two thousand years ago. It is a struggle in which all Americans, non-Jews as well as Jews, should be vitally interested because they are vitally affected.

The Maccabee's victory proved that the Jews—then already an old people—possessed the secret of eternal youth; the ability to rejuvenate itself through courage, hope, enthusiasm, devotion and self-sacrifice of the plain people. This will bring again a Jewish Renaissance.

Louis D. Brandeis
(from an address delivered in Boston, 1912)

NER LI*

Lyrically

Neir— li— neir li neir— li da - kik ba - cha - nu - ka nei - ri ad -

lik ba - cha - nu - ka nei - ri ya - ir ba - cha - nu - ka shi - rim a -

shir la la la la la.............................. ba - cha - nu -

ka nei - ri ya - ir ba - cha - nu - ka shi - rim a - shir

There's a tiny candle
Glowing in the night
Shining in the window
It gives a special light
On Hanukkah it seems to say
"Thank you O Lord
For this special day."

Lyrics © by L. Kipnis; Music by D. Sambursky, © by Tarbut Vechinuch ED., ACUM, Israel.

*See music on page 117.

Hanukkah was once a festival noted for its simplicity and celebrated without fanfare, with the lighting of the Hanukkah menorah (the *hanukiyah*) and the distribution of a few coins of Hanukkah *gelt* (money). Today, more elaborate gift-giving, parties, and home decorations mark its celebration.

Above: This hanukiyah *features the lions of Judah. Below: An eighteenth-century* hanukiyah *from Frankfurt.*

THE RITUAL OF THE HANUKKAH LIGHTS

The sole ritual associated with Hanukkah is the lighting of the eight-branch *hanukiyah*. A seven-branch menorah cannot be used, because that menorah was sacred and exclusive to the Temple. A ninth candle, known as the *shamash* (a servant candle), is used to light the other candles because one candle cannot be used to light another. In fact, all candles are supposed to be on the same level, except for the *shamash*, which is higher, to show that one night is not more important than another.

The schools of the sages of Shammai and Hillel disagreed on how to light the Hanukkah candles. The school of Shammai thought that all eight candles should be lit on the first night and that each night should see one candle less, symbolizing the diminishing oil. The school of Hillel was of the opinion that we should begin with one candle and add an additional candle each night for eight nights, elucidating the principle that we rise rather than descend in holiness. As in most cases, Jewish tradition follows the teachings of Hillel.

The *hanukiyah* used to be placed outside the home for all to see, to publicize the miracle of Hanukkah. Today, Hanukkah menorahs are placed inside the home, near windows, for the same reason.

Hanukkah is a particularly delightful holiday, easy to observe, with few restrictions. It is a holiday especially geared toward children, with delicious fried foods such as potato latkes, fruit fritters, and jelly doughnuts to look forward to; games, such as dreidel, to play; and gifts to give and receive. Although the Rabbis generally disapproved of cards, gambling, and games of chance, these pastimes became popular on Hanukkah.

But underlying the fun of Hanukkah lies a serious message that speaks of courage and action in the face of challenge. From the Maccabees, who defended themselves on the Sabbath, comes the rabbinic ruling that the Sabbath is given to man, not man to the Sabbath, that Judaism's laws were to live by, not to die by. Hanukkah's message teaches that Judaism has to be faithful to its own traditions and must withstand assimilationist pulls and destructive cultural forces. In the end, Hellenism did not consume Judaism; rather, Judaism was influenced by some of the best of Hellenistic thought and became all the more enduring as a result.

TRADITIONS AND CUSTOMS ASSOCIATED WITH HANUKKAH

- It is customary for each member of a household to have her or his own *hanukiyah* and light it each night of the holiday just after sundown.
- According to the Talmud, women, as well as men, are enjoined to kindle the Hanukkah lights.
- There is a tradition for women not to do any work while the Hanukkah lights are burning. Today, this tradition is often observed by both sexes.
- Candles should be tall enough to burn for at least a half hour, and each light should be distinct and not merge with another. On Shabbat eve, the Hanukkah candles are lit just before the Shabbat candles, a half hour before sunset, and should be thick enough to last a half hour after sunset.
- Any clear and clean oil and a wick may be used in the appropriate *hanukiyah*, but olive oil is the oil of preference, for that was the oil used in the Temple.
- The lights from the candles or oil cannot be used for any other purpose (for example, reading or sewing).
- Joy is a hallmark of Hanukkah. It is customary not to mourn or fast during Hanukkah.
- Giving Hanukkah *gelt* (money), and exchanging gifts during Hanukkah. In Israel, gift-giving is not extensive or elaborate.
- The dreidel (or *trendel*), a spinning top, known in Hebrew as the *s'vivon*, is played. Its four letters are *nun* (נ), *gimel* (ג), *hay* (ה), and *shin* (ש), standing for the Hebrew words *"nes gadol hayah sham—"* a great miracle happened there." In Israel, the letter *shin* is replaced by the letter *peh* (פ), meaning "here." Thus, "a great miracle happened here."

- Adding a prayer called *al hanissim* to the Grace after Meals and to the *Amidah* prayer in services during the week of Hanukkah, and reciting the complete *Hallel* each day.
- Singing *Maoz Tzur* (Rock of Ages) after lighting the Hanukkah candles and reciting the blessings. Written by a man called Mordechai in the thirteenth century, its melody is derived from a German folk song and a church hymn. Sephardic Jews recite Psalm 30.
- Eating foods fried in oil, particularly potato latkes and doughnuts, as a reminder of the miracle of the oil.
- In Israel a torch is carried by relay from the city of Modiin to other parts of the country.

Hiddur Mitzvah (Enhancing the Holiday)

There are several ways to enhance the Hanukkah festival. Beautiful and artistic Hanukkah menorahs are available in a variety of materials and designs. Lovely and unusual multicolored candles can be found in some specialty shops and Jewish gift stores. Different kinds of pancakes fried in oil can be added to the Hanukkah menu each night, including carrot, cauliflower, zucchini, cottage cheese, sweet potato, apple, and tuna. Any rolled-cookie recipe can be adapted to make Hanukkah cookies, which children can cut with cookie cutters of Jewish stars, Hanukkah menorahs, and dreidels, and decorate.

HOW TO PLAY DREIDEL

Each player receives an equal number of coins, nuts, raisins, or candies. Each player puts one of these into the middle, or kitty. One person at a time spins the dreidel. The Hebrew letter that it falls upon determines what should be done.

- *Nun* means *nicht* in Yiddish, or nothing: the player does nothing.
- *Gimmel* means *gantz* in Yiddish, or everything: the player takes everything in the kitty.
- *Hay* means *halb* in Yiddish, or half: the player takes half the kitty, or half plus one if there is an odd number in the middle.
- *Shin* means *shtel* in Yiddish, or put in: the player adds something to the kitty.

When nothing is left in the middle, everyone adds something. When a player is out of coins, nuts, raisins, or candies, that player is out of the game. When one person has won everything from the other players, the game is over.

Variations

1. A point value from zero to ten is assigned to each of the four letters on the dreidel. For example, *nun* may be worth zero, while *gimel* may be worth ten points, *shin* two points, and *hay* six points. A caller, who is also the scorekeeper, first spins the dreidel and calls out the letter that the dreidel lands on. Each player in turn spins a dreidel. If it falls on the same letter as the caller's, the player is credited with the points assigned to that letter. If not, he or she receives no points. The first person to reach a stipulated number of points wins.
2. Each player spins the dreidel and gets a numerical value for each turn based on the dreidel's letters and their Hebrew numerical equivalent: ג = 50, ג = 3, ה = 5, and ש = 300. The winner is the one with the highest score after an agreed-upon number of rounds.

3. Each person spins the dreidel and is timed by a stopwatch. The person whose dreidel spins the longest gets a point for that round. The winner is the first person to reach ten points or the highest score.
4. Before the regular dreidel game, about a dozen walnuts are carefully halved with a knife, and the contents of the shell are removed and replaced with a coin or a dollar bill and resealed with Krazy Glue. These walnuts are mixed with the others. After a ten-minute game, the walnuts are opened with a nutcracker, with many surprises. (This idea comes from Susie Wolfson, the wife of Dr. Ron Wolfson, author of *The Art of Jewish Living: Hanukkah*.)

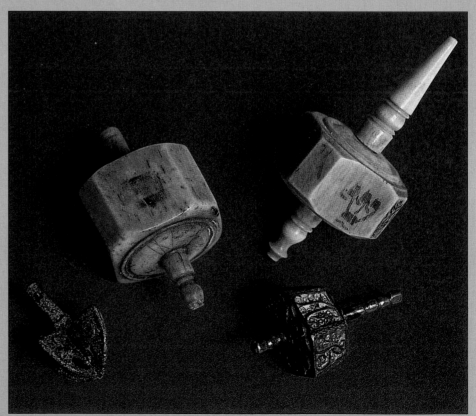

Dreidels comes in many shapes and sizes. Playing dreidel is a favorite Hanukkah pastime.

Children take turns playing dreidel.

ROCK OF AGES— MAOZ TZUR*

Liturgy   **Traditional**

Ma-oz   tzur   y'- shu-a-ti   l'- cha na- eh   l'-sha-bei - ach

Ti-kon   beit t'-fi- la-ti   v'- sham to-da n'- za- bei - ach   L'-

eit   ta-chin, mat- bei- ach   mi-tzar ham'- na- bei - ach

Az   eg-mor   b'shir   miz - mor   cha - nu- kat   ha - miz - bei - ach

Az   eg-mor   b' shir miz - mor   cha - nu- kat ha - miz bei - ach

Rock of ages, let our song
Praise Thy saving power.
Thou amidst the raging foes
Wast our sheltering tower.
Furious they assailed us,
But Thine arm availed us.
And Thy word broke their sword
When our own strength failed us.

*See music on page 117.

HANUKA, HANUKA*

Joyously

Ha - nu - ka   Ha - nu - ka   o-cho— di - yas di fe - li - si - ta
Ha - nu - ka

Ha - nu - ka   o - cho— di - yas di fe - li - si - ta
lai lai lai lai ,lai ,lai lai lai lai lai   lai lai lai lai lai lai

la   lai lai lai lai lai lai   lai lai lai lai   lai lai lai lai lai lai
lai lai lai lai lai lai

lai—lai lai lai lai lai lai   lai lai lai lai lai lai   lai

Hanukah, Hanukah
Eight days of happiness

Hanukah, Hanukah
Eight days of singing

Hanukah, Hanukah
Eight days of dancing

Hanukah, Hanukah
Eight days of enjoying

Sephardic Hannukkah song. © Music and lyrics by Flory Jagoda.

*See music on page 117.

Dreidels (spinning tops), coins (gelt), and potato pancakes (latkes) are an inseparable part of the Hanukkah celebration.

HANUKKAH MENU

There are no formal festive meals for Hanukkah, but foods fried in oil are traditional. For Ashkenazic Jews, these include latkes (potato pancakes) served with applesauce or sour cream, and for Israelis, *sufganiyot* (jelly doughnuts). I especially like making rosettes—a flaky pastry made with a special iron, which are fried in oil and dipped in sugar. There is also a tradition to serve dairy food, particularly those made with cheese, because of Judith, a charming Jewish widow who risked her life to save her town from Holofernes, a general who wanted to destroy it. While dining with him, she fed him cheese, which made him thirsty for wine. This put him to sleep. It was while he was asleep that Judith beheaded him, causing his soldiers to flee in fear and thereby saving the town.

Butternut Squash Soup
Israeli Salad
Pan-Glazed Apples with Old-Fashioned Potato Latkes
or Cauliflower Pancakes
Broiled Ginger Salmon
Jelly Doughnuts
Ice Cream with Chocolate Sauce
Rosettes
Fresh Fruit: Mandarin Oranges or Clementines

Butternut Squash Soup

This velvety sweet squash soup is adapted from a recipe sent to me by Peter Graben, of Peter Graben Caterers of Toronto, Canada.

- 3 tablespoons unsalted butter or sweet pareve margarine
- 2 finely chopped medium yellow or Vidalia onions
- 1 large butternut squash (about 2½ pounds)
- 2 Golden Delicious apples, peeled and chopped
- 4 to 5 cups vegetable stock or water, or 4 teaspoons kosher pareve low-sodium chicken-flavored soup mix dissolved in 4 or 5 cups hot water
- 1⅓ cups apple juice
- ¼ teaspoon nutmeg
- Dash of cinnamon
- Dash of allspice
- Salt and freshly ground pepper to taste

Melt the margarine in a saucepan. Add chopped onions and cook covered over low heat until onion is translucent. Peel the squash, remove seeds, and chop in food processor or cube by hand. Add squash and apples to the onions and sauté 1 minute. Add half of chicken stock and bring to a boil. Reduce heat and simmer about 20 minutes until squash and apples are tender.

Put the squash mixture in a blender or food processor or use a hand blender and blend until smooth. Return squash mixture to saucepan. Add rest of stock, apple juice, and spices. Add more stock for thinner consistency, if desired. Season to taste with salt and pepper. Heat but do not boil. Garnish with sliced apple or cinnamon stick.

Serves 6 to 8.

Butternut Squash Soup.

Israeli Salad

This light Israeli salad adds a healthy touch to the not-so-healthy fried foods of Hanukkah! It also is a reminder that the Hanukkah story took place in Israel.

- 2 cucumbers, diced
- 4 tomatoes, diced
- 6 scallions, chopped
- 2 green peppers, diced
- Salt to taste
- Freshly ground black pepper
- Juice of 2 lemons
- ⅓ cup olive oil

Combine vegetables in a bowl. Season to taste and add lemon juice and olive oil. Toss gently.

Serves 8.

Pan-Glazed Apples

- 4 or 5 medium tart red or green apples
- 3 tablespoons butter or margarine
- ¼ to ⅓ cup sugar, depending on apple tartness
- 3 tablespoons apple juice
- ¼ teaspoon cinnamon
- ¼ teaspoon nutmeg
- ¼ teaspoon cloves

Core and cut apples into thin wedges. It is unnecessary to peel apples, but if desired, peel them before cutting. Heat margarine in skillet. Add apples, sugar, juice, cinnamon, nutmeg, and cloves. Cover and simmer for 3 to 5 minutes. Uncover and cook 5 more minutes or until apples are glazed and tender, but not mushy.

Serves 6 to 8.

Old-Fashioned Potato Pancakes (Latkes)

This latke recipe came to me from Susan Mandelbaum of Livingston, New Jersey. She insists that the secret to latkes is draining them well, and using Crisco® oil.

- 3 cups grated Idaho potatoes
- 1 onion, grated
- 3 scallions, chopped with greens
- 2 eggs, beaten well
- ½ cup matzo meal
- 1½ teaspoons salt, or to taste
- Freshly ground pepper
- Oil for frying

In food processor or with a medium-blade grater, grate potatoes. Then grate onion and place in a separate bowl. Rinse with cold water and drain *thoroughly*, squeezing out all liquid. Pat dry with paper towels. Add grated onion and chopped scallions into well-drained potatoes. Add beaten eggs, matzo meal, salt, and pepper and mix well. Heat oil until hot. Drop potato mixture into pan by tablespoonful. Even out with a knife. Fry until brown and turn over. Drain on paper towels. Keep warm by placing on foil-lined cookie sheet in a warm oven. Serve with sour cream or pan glazed apples.

   To freeze, place on a single layer in cookie sheet. Pop into freezer. When frozen, remove with spatula, place into freezer bag, and freeze.

Yields about 16 pancakes.

Note: For vegetable latkes, use a combination of potatoes, carrots, and zucchini to make 3 cups of vegetables.

Old-Fashioned Potato Pancakes.

Broiled Ginger Salmon.

Cauliflower Pancakes

These tasty pancakes from Annalee Richler of Toronto are a delightful change from potato latkes. The cheddar cheese is especially appropriate for Hanukkah, when there is a tradition to eat dairy, particularly cheese, dishes.

- ½ large head cauliflower
- 1 small onion
- 1 tablespoon vegetable oil
- 2 eggs
- 2 tablespoons milk
- ¼ cup plus 1 tablespoon flour
- ¾ teaspoon baking powder
- ½ teaspoon salt
- ¼ teaspoon freshly ground pepper
- ½ cup grated cheese
- Oil for frying

Steam cauliflower until tender. While cauliflower is steaming, sauté onion in 1 tablespoon vegetable oil. Set aside. Cut steamed cauliflower into bite-size pieces. Mix eggs, milk, flour, baking powder, salt, pepper, cheese, and sautéed onion until smooth. Add cauliflower to the batter and mix well. Heat 1 inch of oil until hot. Drop mixture by tablespoonful into hot oil and cook until golden brown on each side. Drain well on paper towels.

Makes about 12 pancakes.

Note: Broccoli can be substituted for cauliflower.

Broiled Ginger Salmon

Lawrence Jay of Lawrence David Jay Caterers of Garwood, New Jersey, generously shared this easy and delicious salmon recipe with me.

- 3 pounds fillet of salmon

Marinade
- 4½ tablespoons chopped scallions
- 3 tablespoons fresh grated ginger
- 1 tablespoon oil
- ¼ cup soy sauce
- 1 teaspoon mirin (an Asian sweet rice wine), sherry, or white wine
- 1 teaspoon sesame oil
- 1 tablespoon sugar
- ⅛ teaspoon white pepper

Sauté scallions and ginger in oil 2 to 3 minutes, until golden brown. Combine remaining ingredients. Marinate fish from 1 hour to overnight. Broil fish on one side until brown and glazed. Transfer to platter.

Serves 6 to 8.

Jelly Doughnuts (Sufganiyot)

Jelly doughnuts are popular among Israelis on Hanukkah. Making them yourself may be some work, but it can be fun as well. Try a variety of jellies.

- 2 packages active dry yeast
- ½ cup warm water
- ½ cup milk or nondairy creamer
- ¼ cup sugar
- 1 teaspoon salt
- ⅓ cup butter or pareve margarine
- 2 eggs plus 1 egg yolk
- 1 teaspoon nutmeg
- ½ teaspoon cinnamon
- 3½ cups flour
- 1 egg white, lightly beaten
- ⅓ cup jelly or jam of your choice
- Oil for deep frying
- Confectioners' sugar or granulated sugar

Dissolve yeast in warm water in a large bowl. Set aside. Heat milk (or nondairy creamer) until hot but not boiling. Remove from heat. Add sugar, salt, and butter or margarine and stir until melted. Cool until warm to the touch. Add to yeast mixture along with eggs and yolk, nutmeg, cinnamon, and 2 cups of the flour. Beat with electric mixer until smooth. Beat in remaining flour by hand until smooth. Knead a minute, adding a little more flour if necessary. Cover with towel and let rise in a warm place until doubled in bulk, about 1 hour.

Punch down dough and knead a minute or two on a floured board until smooth and elastic. Let rest about 10 minutes. Roll on floured board until ¼ inch thick.

Cut into 2½-inch rounds using doughnut or biscuit cutter or glass. Place a teaspoon of jam or jelly on a circle and brush with egg white. Place another circle on top and press edges together to seal. Repeat with remainder of dough.

Place on lightly floured board or cookie sheet and cover with towel. Let rise until doubled in bulk, about 1 hour.

In heavy pot or skillet, heat 2 inches of oil until 360 degrees F. Gently drop

Ice Cream with Chocolate Sauce.

doughnuts into hot oil. Fry a few doughnuts at a time and turn until they rise to the surface. Fry until golden brown, about 1 to 2 minutes per side. Remove with slotted spoon and drain on paper towel.

Dust with sifted confectioners' sugar or granulated sugar. Serve as soon as possible.

Makes 16 to 18 doughnuts.

Chocolate Sauce

This easy chocolate sauce is wonderful on ice cream or a pareve (nondairy) dessert. Because it contains no corn syrup, it can be adapted for Passover use as well.

- 2 tablespoons margarine
- 2 ounces unsweetened chocolate
- 1 cup sugar
- Pinch of salt
- ½ cup water
- 1 teaspoon vanilla
- ½ teaspoon of cinnamon
- 1 tablespoon chocolate-flavored liqueur (optional)

In a saucepan, melt margarine and chocolate together. Add remaining ingredients. Cook over low heat until desired thickness is reached. Serve warm or cool. Can be refrigerated and warmed in the microwave.

Makes 1 cup.

Rosettes

Rosettes for Hanukkah were introduced to me by Pearl Smock, a talented lady I knew in Alaska. She presented me with a rosette iron and her recipe for these delectable, crispy, and artistic pastries. This is a variation of her recipe.

- 2 eggs
- 2 tablespoons sugar
- 1 cup flour
- Dash of salt
- 1 cup water or milk
- 2 teaspoons lemon extract
- Confectioners' sugar

Mix all ingredients with a wire whisk or in a blender. Strain batter if desired. Let rest ½ hour. Pour into a bowl.

Heat 2 inches of oil in a small, heavy pot to 370 degrees F. Heat rosette iron in oil for about 10 seconds. Tap excess oil from iron. Dip the hot iron into the batter, just until it is on top of the edge of the iron, but not over it. Immediately dip the iron and batter into hot oil and fry for 15 to 20 seconds or until delicately browned. Lift iron out and tip to drain. Remove rosette from iron with a fork. Stir batter each time before dipping iron. Again, dip iron in oil and repeat with remaining batter, reheating iron each time. Sprinkle rosettes with granulated or confectioners' sugar.

Makes about 36 rosettes.

CHAPTER FIVE

PURIM

"With the arrival of the month of Adar, joy is increased," states the Talmud. This is in anticipation of the merry holiday of Purim, which takes place in the middle of the Hebrew month of Adar, on the fourteenth day of the month.

Purim, like Hanukkah, is considered a minor holiday in the Jewish calendar, in contrast to the pilgrimage festivals of Pesah, Shavuot, and Sukkot, and the High Holy Days, which are major holidays. Work does not cease, nor are there any of the usual holiday restrictions on Purim.

Minor holiday though it may be, Purim has nonetheless captured a major place in Jewish minds and hearts. Purim, like Hanukkah, is a holiday of deliverance: Hanukkah celebrates the deliverance of the Jewish people from forces that tried to snuff out Jewish spiritual life; Purim celebrates the physical deliverance of the Jewish people from a tyrant bent on their physical destruction.

HISTORICAL ACCURACY OF PURIM

Although the historicity of the holiday has been called into question by scholars who challenge the authenticity of the persons and the events described in the Scroll of Esther, Jews themselves seem to have settled the scholarly debate by their sentimental and unconditional attachment to this almost secular holiday. It is a holiday like no other in the Jewish calendar, with its unabashed joy, mirth, old-fashioned fun, and sense of absurdity.

The Purim story in the Scroll of Esther reads like a historical novel. It seems to matter not whether the events described actually took place, whether the foolish Ahasuerus is Xerxes I (486–465 B.C.E.) or Artaxerxes II (404–359 B.C.E.), whether the names of Mordecai and Esther derive from the Babylonian gods Marduk and Ishtar, as they most probably do, or whether a pagan holiday preceded Purim. What is important is what this holiday has represented for Jews in years past and present. As Elie Wiesel has written, "Some events do take place but are not true; others are—although they never occurred." There is an eternal truth to the story of Esther that defies time and place and even actuality.

Opposite: Purim wall decoration depicting scenes from the Scroll of Esther, created by Sara Eydel Weissburg of Jerusalem. Above: Woodcut of Purim jesters from Sefer Minhagim, the Book of Customs, Venice, 1593.

The architect of the Purim story is not God, for there is no mention of God in the Megillah, or of any kind of Divine intervention, although for the Rabbis, and certainly for the kabbalists (sixteenth-century Jewish mystics), Divine intervention was assumed. On the surface, the heroes of the story, Mordecai and Esther, avert disaster by saving the Jewish people. Deliverance comes about as a result of human courage and initiative, not *deus ex machina*, or Divine mediation.

BIGTHAN AND TERESH ARE DEAD

On Fortune's cap we are not the very button...
(*Hamlet*, Act II, Scene II)

The world of literature is filled with many minor characters caught up in the larger drama of the real heroes and heroines. These minor characters either move the plot along, serve as humorous diversions, or remind the reader that chamberlains in the employ of a king can be caught unawares in schemes that transcend their own conspiracies. So it is with Bigthan and Teresh.

These two courtiers to King Ahasuerus are usually depicted as laughable buffoons, a kind of gang that couldn't shoot straight, who tried to kill the king and cast suspicion upon Mordecai. This hapless duo were caught in their plot to assassinate King Ahasuerus by Mordecai, who reported the plot to Esther. Esther told the king and Bigthan and Teresh were executed. Mordecai's discovery of the plot was duly noted in the daily logs of the king, but Mordecai was not honored, and the incident was seemingly forgotten.

Yet Bigthan and Teresh, like Rosencrantz and Guildenstern, deserve more than just a footnote. After all, it was their bumbling conspiracy uncovered by Mordecai that propelled the Purim story forward and trapped Haman in a downward spiral that eventually led to his demise.

Several midrashic sources imply that Bigthan and Teresh were Macedonians whose allegiances were to Greece. At the time, the Persians were at war with Greece, and Bigthan and Teresh wanted the Persian empire to fall to the Greeks. Haman, a Greek himself, was the original author of the plot against Ahasuerus. And Haman aspired to kingship. What better way to attain his goal than to assassinate the king, have Persia fall to the Greeks, and have himself emerge as the hero of Greek nationalism?

But Mordecai, who overheard the plot, was a Jew loyal to the Persian empire. Haman's plot was thwarted by Mordecai, and so his wrath against Mordecai grew. Haman, a traitor to Ahasuerus and Persia, projected his own treasonous proclivities not just to Mordecai but to all the Jews, accusing them of a dual loyalty of which he, himself, was guilty.

And poor Bigthan and Teresh, little cogs in a larger wheel of conspiracies, were unaware of the large stakes in the game that was being played. Thus, these minor characters came to a bad end, a footnote in a larger story, while Mordecai, loyal to his king and country, honest, straight and true, rose to become prime minister. His people remained faithful subjects to an empire that would eventually allow the Jews to return to their native land and rebuild their temple.

THE PLOT

The story of the Book of Esther plays out like a grade "B" movie. It is a tale of power and intrigue, of plots and counterplots, thwarted schemes, romance, and bravery with a Hollywood-type ending of deliverance and retribution.

It is the story of a fatuous king of Persia, Ahasuerus, who summons his wife, Vashti, to a banquet. She rejects his bidding, and after consulting with his advisers, he orders her banishment. After a time, he holds a beauty contest to choose his next queen. He selects a beautiful Jewish maiden named Esther (Hadassah), who hides her identity as a Jew. Esther's protector and guardian, her cousin Mordecai, overhears a plan to assassinate the king, and tells Esther, who promptly warns the king of the plot, which is then foiled. The deed is recorded in a book of chronicles.

Meanwhile, the wicked vizier to the king, Haman, is bent upon promoting himself. When Mordecai refuses to bow

In this engraving, Esther is chosen queen by King Ahashuerus and bestowed his crown.

down to him and accord him the deference that he thinks is his due, Haman becomes incensed and seeks revenge by plotting to destroy the entire Jewish population of Persia. He does so by convincing the simpleminded and gullible king that the Jews pose an internal threat, since they are a people apart. Having been granted permission to proceed with his plan, Haman decides to exterminate the Jews on the fourteenth of Adar, based on lots (purim) cast—from whence we get the name of the holiday.

Mordecai, upon discovering Haman's evil intentions, decides to intervene by convincing Esther that it is her duty as a Jew to expose Haman and thwart his evil scheme. Esther fasts for three days before embarking on her dangerous mission. She goes to the king, inviting him and Haman to a party in her chambers.

That night, the king is restless, and reads the book of chronicles that recorded Mordecai's act of loyalty to the king. The king discovers that Mordecai has never been rewarded for his extraordinary deed and asks Haman how such a person is to be recompensed. Haman, assuming that it is he himself who is to be handsomely rewarded, suggests that the king's benefactor be led through the streets of Shushan dressed in royal clothing on the king's horse. Haman, to his horror, is the one designated to lead the procession to honor Mordecai.

At Esther's sumptuous feast, where wine and food flow freely, Esther entices the king and Haman to visit her again the next day. At that time, Esther exposes Haman for the villain he is, and reveals her true identity. The infuriated king orders Haman's hanging upon the very gallows meant for Mordecai.

The Jews are granted not just a stay of execution, but the right to self-defense, and they fight and defeat their enemies. A holiday for feasting and gladness is established by Mordecai and Esther to be commemorated each year on the fourteenth of Adar by the giving of gifts to one another, as well as to the poor.

In Shushan, the capital of Persia, the celebration takes place on the fifteenth of Adar, because the Jews there fought an additional day. In Jerusalem, Purim is celebrated on the fifteenth of the month, because, like Shushan, Jerusalem is a walled city. This is in keeping with the rabbinic ruling that all walled cities at the time of Joshua should observe Shushan Purim.

Haman leading Mordecai through the streets of Shushan.

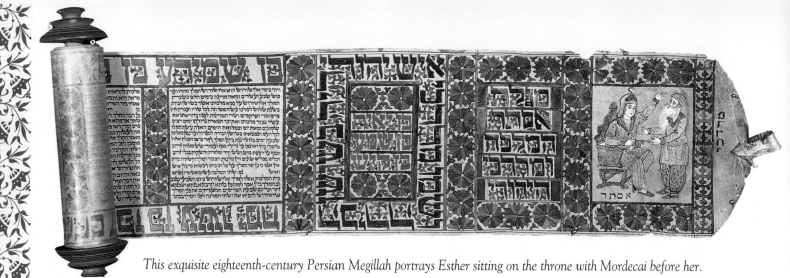

This exquisite eighteenth-century Persian Megillah portrays Esther sitting on the throne with Mordecai before her.

IN SHU, SHU, SHUSHAN*

Lyrics: R. Learsi. Music adapted and arranged by Harry Coopersmith

In a jolly manner

Oh Ha-man was a high and might-y bluff, In Shu-shu Shu shan long a-go He or-dered Morde-cai to take his der-by off In Shu-shu shu-shan long a-go.

Chorus
So we sing, so we sing! so we sing and raise a row! For Ha-man he was swing-ing, while Mor de-cai was sing-ing, In Shu-shu shu-shan long a-go.

But Mordecai sat and laughed in his face
In Shu, shu, Shushan long ago.
So Haman swore he'd exterminate his race
In Shu, Shu Shushan long ago.

Chorus

O Esther was a timid little maid
In Shu, Shu Shushan long ago.
But Mordecai told her she needn't be afraid
In Shu, Shu Shushan long ago.

Chorus

So she went to the king and she gave him a smile
In Shu, Shu Shushan long ago.
The king he liked her manner and her style
In Shu, Shu Shushan long ago.

Chorus

Ahasuerus was a jolly little king
In Shu, Shu Shushan long ago.
He ordered Haman to take a little swing
In Shu, Shu Shushan long ago.

Chorus

From *The Songs We Sing* edited by Harry Coopersmith. © 1950 by the United Synagogue of America, with permission.

*See music on page 118.

THE MEGILLAH

Handwritten on parchment and sometimes illustrated, the Scroll of Esther, *Megillat Esther*, is the best known of the *megillot* found in Holy Scripture. So closely linked are the Scroll of Esther and Purim, that one without the other is unthinkable and no explanation is necessary to connect the two. This is unlike *megillot* read on other Jewish holidays (Song of Songs on Passover; Ruth on Shavuot; Lamentations on Tisha B'Av; and Ecclesiastes on Sukkot), where the relationship between the holiday and the *megillah* is not always as apparent and is sometimes even tenuous. In fact, the capitalized word *Megillah* invariably refers only to the Book of Esther. In current practice, the Scroll of Esther is the only *megillah* read with blessings.

Before the reading of the *Megillah*, three blessings are recited, and a special cantillation, particular to the *Megillah* of Esther, is used. A blessing is also recited after the reading. Women, as well as men, are obliged to hear the *Megillah*, which is read both at night and on the day of Purim. The scroll is

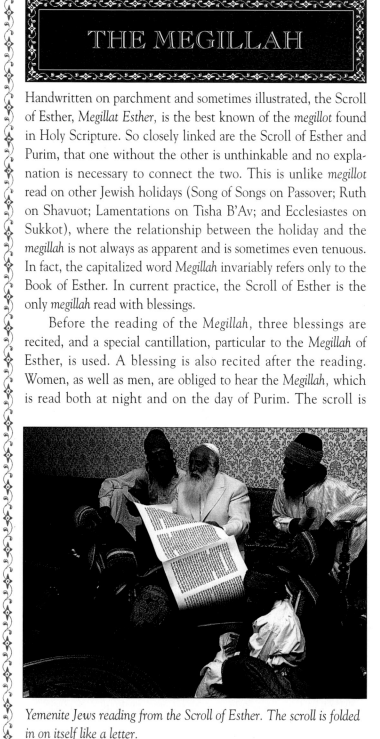

Yemenite Jews reading from the Scroll of Esther. The scroll is folded in on itself like a letter.

unrolled and folded back upon itself like a letter, because letters were sent to all the Jews of Persia by Mordecai and Esther promulgating the holiday.

A special meal is eaten on the day of Purim in the afternoon, known as *Seudat Purim*. But no traditional holiday kiddush is recited, nor are candles lit, for Purim is, at its core, not a religious holiday. One of the days Purim never falls on Shabbat.

ANTI-SEMITISM IN THE PURIM STORY

Purim appeals to every Jewish generation, for the story of Purim at its most basic is the archetypical tale of anti-Semitism in its rawest and barest form. It is a tale of evil that periodically rears its ugly head. It is the all-too-hauntingly familiar story of the experience of Diaspora Jewry. Haman represents an implacable foe whose unrelenting hatred for the Jew, taken to its extreme, finds its ultimate expression in violence, murder, and genocide. It is only because of a fortuitous turn of events that Persian Jewry is spared, and that Jews around the world symbolically obliterate Haman's name with the stamping of feet and sounding of noisemakers, known as gragers, instead of being obliterated themselves.

If Haman represents unmitigated evil, Ahasuerus represents the indifferent and naive individual who is all too easily influenced and who, with the stroke of a pen, can doom a people without being aware of the consequences of his actions. Esther represents courage that conquers fear, and cleverness that joins forces with ingenuity with impressive results. Mordecai is the honorable Jew who conducts himself with aplomb and integrity and receives his just reward.

PARODY AND PLAYS

Therefore, for Jews, Purim is a symbolic as well as a cathartic experience. The Rabbis instinctively understood this, and even encouraged an emotional release. Barriers and defenses came down on Purim; rules were relaxed. Inebriation was encouraged, irreverence delighted in, sacred cows gleefully profaned. Humor and burlesque were freely used on Purim—welcome contrasts to the highly disciplined and regulated quality of everyday Jewish life. *Purim spiels* (plays) became the order of the day, along with *Purim Torah* (poking fun at and spoofing rabbis and their sacred traditions and texts) and an impressive literature of satire and parody grew. Carnivals borrowed from Italian (or Christian) celebrations were adapted by Jews to celebrate this joyous holiday, as were masks and masquerades.

Purim Midrash

The rabbinic imagination, always fruitful, exploded with the rich possibilities of the Purim story—more so than with almost any other holiday. There is a wealth of Aggadic (pertaining to midrash) material in connection with the Purim story.

For example, according to the midrash (rabbinic commentary, legend, and lore), Ahasuerus was not the king by dint of birth, but because of his vast wealth. He was so rich that no drinking cup was used more than once. The name Mordecai consists of the word *mor* (myrrh) and *decai* (Aramaic, meaning "pure"), for Mordecai, who hailed from Jerusalem nobility, was as

AMALEK: THE ETERNAL ENEMY

No nation evinced as much bitterness toward the Israelites as did the Amalekites. The ancient Israelites long remembered how this brutal tribe attacked women, children, the aged, and the sick as they wandered through the wilderness (Deut. 25:17–19). The name Amalek became synonymous with evil, and the Israelites were commanded to "blot out the memory of Amalek from under the heaven."

It was not until the period of King Saul, whose father was Kish and who came from the tribe of Benjamin, that there was an opportunity to deal a final blow to the Amalekites. Unfortunately, King Saul was unable to completely destroy the Amalekites; they survived only to haunt Israel and become the personification of evil.

When Haman's pedigree is identified in the Scroll of Esther, he is known as the "Agagite" (Esther 3:1), the name given to the last king of the Amalekites captured under Saul. When Mordecai's pedigree is identified, he is known as a descendant of "Kish, a Benjaminite" (Esther 2:5), the father of Saul.

The author of the Scroll of Esther has stunningly brought together these two protagonists to finish what could not be done a

thousand years earlier. The victory of light over darkness, of righteousness over wickedness could now be played out between Mordecai and Haman. For Jews, the Amalekites and Haman became metaphors for a wicked people or individual, respectively, whose hatred of Jews was implacable.

The author of the Scroll of Esther brilliantly wove together elements of ancient Israelite history by plucking out the unfinished business between Saul and the Amalekites, as described in the First Book of Samuel, Chapter 15, and projecting that clash between Amalek and Israel against the backdrop of the story of Esther.

On the Sabbath before Purim, Shabbat Zakhor (the Sabbath of Remembrance), a special section from the Torah is read, reminding Israel to remember Amalek, and the Haftarah is the story of Saul and his failure to destroy this wicked and vicious tribe.

The struggle between good and evil never ceases, and so the world of Amalek and Haman are still mentioned by Jews everywhere when they want to identify a people who seeks to destroy them, or an individual who hates them.

fine and worthy as myrrh. Esther's birth resulted in her mother's death, and she was brought up by Mordecai. Her Hebrew name, Hadassah, means myrtle, because her good deeds permeated everywhere like the scent of myrtle. Esther was also like a myrtle, which has an acrid taste despite its wonderful fragrance. Esther was gracious to her fellow Jews, but sharp to Haman. These are but a few of the creative ways the Rabbis explored and interpreted the Scroll of Esther.

PURIM AND YOM KIPPUR

Although the Rabbis were permissive and indulgent toward Purim, they were nonetheless able to remove the holiday's masks and masquerades and penetrate beneath the surface. Tearing away at Purim's outer layers, the kabbalists unmasked the essence of the holiday itself by pronouncing Yom Kippur, also known as Yom Kippurim, as *Yom Ki-Purim*, a day like Purim. The Day of Atonement and Purim would at first glance seem to be two opposites of the Jewish festival spectrum. Yom Kippur is the holiest day of the Jewish year, a day of sanctity and solemnity; Purim is a day of unrestrained revelry and irreverence. Yet both days

represent the Jewish soul and spirit, the laughter and tears, the joy and solemnity that mark the Jewish festivals and their celebration. To the Rabbis, both days were times of fateful decision when an individual's lot could be decided, as on Yom Kippur, or a nation's fate determined, as on Purim. Despite a certain capriciousness, the Purim story appealed to their sense of justice when wrongs were righted, evil dealt a mortal blow, and things turned out as they should.

A JEWISH HOLIDAY

For all its indulgences and excesses Purim has another side as well. Purim remains an essentially Jewish holiday. There is a reaching out to others as is enjoined in the *Megillah* through the customs of *matanot laevyonim* (gifts to the poor) and *mishloah manot* (gifts to friends). These are the purely Jewish aspects of Purim that do not derive from any other nation or influence. "When all other festivals cease to be observed," says the midrash, "Purim will never be annulled." In that statement, the Rabbis express something profound and eternal about one of the most beloved holidays of the Jewish year.

A Bukharan family in traditional dress celebrates Purim.

TRADITIONS AND CUSTOMS ASSOCIATED WITH PURIM

- Reading of the Scroll of Esther on the evening and day of Purim. According to tradition, women as well as men are obliged to hear and may read the *Megillah* because Esther plays such a pivotal role in the holiday.

- Noisemaking is used to blot out Haman's name. This is done with the use of noisemakers called *graggers* or by other means such as booing, whistle blowing, or stamping one's feet. The names of Haman's ten sons are read in one breath to show that they died together and to quickly run through something distasteful without gloating over one's enemies.

- Burning Haman in effigy used to be a common practice, but is now only done by Sephardic Jews. Some Sephardic Jews write Haman's name on their shoes and blot it out. At one time Jews would draw a picture of Haman on stones and also rub it out.

- The Fast of Esther, known as *Taanit Esther*, recalls how the Jews of Persia fasted before fighting their enemies and takes place on the thirteenth of Adar. This custom is particularly strictly observed by Persian (Iranian) Jews. In another custom, Iranian Jews give children gifts on Purim instead of Hanukkah because Purim falls close to the Iranian *Norouz* or New Year.

- The *Al Hanissim* prayer is added to the Grace after Meals and to the *Amidah* on Purim.

- The traditional food among Ashkenazic Jews is hamantaschen, originally known as *Mohntaschen* (German for "poppy-seed pockets"). The three-cornered filled pastry made of yeast or cookie dough was thought to resemble the three-cornered hat worn by Haman. For the same reason, triangular meat-filled dough pockets called *kreplach* are eaten on Purim.

- A *Seudat Purim*, or festive meal, is held on Purim afternoon, a reminder of the banquets in the Book of Esther.

- *Mishloah manot* or *shalakh manos*: sending at least two kinds of food or goodies to friends is based upon a verse in the Book of Esther (9:22). The tradition is to give *matanot laevyonim*—gifts to at least two poor people. *Mahazit hashekel*, or half shekel, is in commemoration of money given by every Israelite for the Temple's upkeep and is given in the synagogue in the form of three coins (in the United States, usually half dollars) for charity.

- Dressing up in costume (masquerade) is still a common and delightful practice enjoyed by young and old. Purim is the one holiday where men and women were permitted by the Rabbis to dress up in clothes of the opposite sex.

- *Purim spiels*: dramatizations and satirizations of the Purim story date to the sixteenth century and are still performed. So is *Purim Torah*, the parodying of rabbis, Torah, prayers, and scholarship by deliberate misapplications, misinterpretations, and burlesque.

AL HANISSIM FOR PURIM

We thank You for the heroism, for the triumphs, and for the miraculous deliverance of our ancestors, in other days and in our time. In the days of Mordecai and Esther, in Shushan, the capital of Persia, the wicked Haman rose up against all Jews and plotted their destruction. In a single day, the thirteenth of Adar, the twelfth month of the year, Haman planned to annihilate all Jews, young and old, and to permit the plunder of their property. You, in great mercy, thwarted his designs, frustrated his plot, and visited upon him the evil he planned to bring on others. Haman, together with his sons, suffered death on the gallows he had made for Mordecai.

A WICKED MAN*

Folk Song

O once there was a wick-ed wick-ed man and Ha-man was his name, sir. He would have mur-dered all the Jews though they were not to blame sir. O to-day we'll mer-ry mer-ry be O to-day we'll mer-ry mer-ry be O to-day we'll mer-ry mer-ry be and nash some ha-man ta-shen.

And Esther was the lovely queen
Of King Ahashverosh
When Haman said he'd kill us all
O my how he did scare us
O today we'll ....

But Mordecai her cousin bold
Said: "What a dreadful chutzpa!
If guns were but invented now
This Haman I would shoot sir."
O today we'll ....

The guest of honor he shall be
This clever Mr. Smarty
And high above us he shall swing
At a little hanging party
O today we'll ....

Of all his cruel and unkind ways
This little joke did cure him
And don't forget we owe him thanks
For this jolly feast of Purim
O today we'll ....

*See music on page 118.

ANI PURIM*

Allegretto

A - ni Pu - rim a - ni Pu - rim sa - mei - ach um - va - dei - ach ha -

lo rak pa - am ba - sha - na a - vo l' - hit - a - rei - ach la la la la la la la

la la la la la la la la la la la la la la

I am Purim, I am Purim
Happy and of good cheer
If only I could make a visit
More than once a year!

Lyrics by L. Kipnis; music by N. Nardi.
Lyrics © by the author. Music © by Tarbut Vechinuch ED., ACUM, Israel.

*See music on page 118.

PURIM
by Ilo Orleans

Purim Day is a *jolly* day,
  When every Jew rejoices.
Purim Day is a *happy* day
  For laughing hearts and voices.

Purim Day is a *friendly* day,
  A holiday so pleasant,
  That everyone is glad to give,
  And glad to get a present.

Purim Day is a *cheery* day,
  For the fun it's always bringing,
With Purim games and Purim plays,
  And Purim dance and singing!

Purim Day is a *stirring* day.
  We read Queen Esther's story—
Of Mordecai and the Persian king
  In all their ancient glory!

Purim Day is a *festive* day,
  A day for celebrating
Haman's fall—the tyrant, whom
  We never shall stop hating.

Purim Day is a *jolly* day,
  When every Jew rejoices.
Purim Day is a *happy* day
  For laughing hearts and voices.

Reprinted by permission of Karen S. Solomon.

- Drinking is a time-honored Purim tradition. The Rabbis said that one should drink so much as to be unable to distinguish between "Blessed is Mordecai" and "Cursed is Haman."
- Carnivals and parades are popular Purim events. The famous Tel Aviv carnival and parade known as the *Adloyada* takes place each year on Purim and consists of floats, costumes, marchers, dancing, and music.

Hiddur Mitzvah
(Enhancing the Holiday)

Beautiful hand-decorated or ready-made containers, baskets, boxes, or paper plates can be used for *mishloah manot*. The gifts of food can include homemade cookies, different kinds of *hamantaschen*, confections, jams, miniature bottles of wine or liqueurs, juice, candies, salted snacks, fresh and dried fruit, and nuts. Pennies or other coins can also be included.

With a little imagination, makeup, cardboard, crepe paper, and some clothes, wonderful costumes can be created at home for Purim. Anything goes. Aside from the Purim characters of Esther, Mordecai, Haman, and Ahasuerus, dressing up as a clown, troll, circus performer, ballet dancer, queen, king, Indian, Mexican, Spaniard, Dutch girl, Hasid, Arab sheik, bride, groom, animal, flower, storybook or cartoon character, or a famous person are among the endless possibilities.

Children delight in wearing costumes for Purim. A boy dressed up as Moses holds the Ten Commandments.

A Purim seudah, *or banquet, is traditionally served on the afternoon of Purim.*

PURIM MENU

The Purim *seudah*, or banquet, is the festive meal of Purim, usually eaten in the afternoon. The following menu includes a bean dish, because there is a tradition that Esther ate legumes in the Persian court to keep kosher. The triangular pastries known as *hamantaschen* are featured here with a variety of fillings. Best known of these is poppyseed, or *mohn* in German, which sounds like Haman. There is also a refreshing fruit punch that can be made with or without alcohol.

Melon Balls in Honey-Lime Sauce with Easy Pineapple Sorbet

Parsnip and Fennel Soup

Chickpea and Bean Salad

Mushroom Garlic Chicken

Poppy Seed Noodles

Snow Peas, Red Peppers, and Bamboo Shoots

Hamantaschen: Poppy Seed, Plum, Chocolate, and Prune

Ma'amoul

Cranberry Fruit Punch

Melon Balls in Honey-Lime Sauce with Pineapple Sorbet.

Melon Balls in Honey-Lime Sauce

This is an elegant and refreshing way to begin the Purim seudah and still leave room for hamantaschen.

- ½ large honeydew melon
- 1 cantaloupe
- ⅓ cup lime juice
- 3 tablespoons honey
- 1 teaspoon grated lime zest
- 3 tablespoons pineapple juice
- 2 tablespoons Midori® (melon) liqueur (optional)
- 1 cup green grapes

Using a melon baller, scoop out honeydew melon and cantaloupe. Combine lime juice, lime zest, honey, pineapple juice, and liqueur. Mix well and pour over melon. Add grapes. Toss well. Refrigerate for at least 1 hour. Serve in individual dishes and top with a small scoop of pineapple sorbet.

Serves 6 to 8.

Note: Other seasonal melons can be used.

Easy Pineapple Sorbet

The secret to sorbet is to serve it as soon as possible after it is firm. Sorbet is best on the day it is made.

- 1½ cups fresh or canned pineapple (20-ounce can, drained)
- ½ cup superfine or instant granulated sugar
- 2 tablespoons lemon juice
- 2 cups of water

In a food processor, puree the pineapple, sugar, and lemon juice. In a glass or plastic bowl, stir in the pineapple mixture with the water. Freeze until solid—about two to three hours. Break into chunks and return to food processor bowl. Process only until smooth. Freeze just until firm—about 15 minutes. If sorbet gets too hard, process in food processor and freeze for an hour or two before serving. Sorbet can be made in an ice cream maker.

Parsnip and Fennel Soup

This light and smooth soup is a recipe from my sister Laurie Gottlieb of Montreal, Canada.

- 2 tablespoons pareve margarine
- 1 large onion, diced
- 3 large parsnips, scraped and cubed (1 pound)
- ½ large fennel bulb (anise), sliced
- 6 cups chicken broth
- 2 tablespoons nondairy creamer
- ½ teaspoon curry (optional)
- 1 tablespoon fresh lemon juice
- Lemon slices
- Dill sprigs

Melt margarine in a heavy saucepan. Add onion, parsnips, and fennel and stir to coat with margarine. Cook for 5 minutes over low heat. Boil chicken broth and add to vegetables. Cook over low heat until vegetables are soft, about 30 minutes. In a food processor or blender, puree vegetables and liquid. Return to pot. Add creamer, curry, and lemon juice. Correct seasoning. Reheat until hot, but do not bring to a boil. Ladle into soup bowls.

To garnish, place a sprig of dill on a thin lemon slice, and float the lemon on top of the soup.

Serves 6 to 8.

Chickpea and Bean Salad

- ½ pound green beans, trimmed
- ½ pound yellow beans, trimmed
- 1 cup canned chickpeas, rinsed and drained
- ½ cup fresh shelled sweet peas
- ½ pound snow peas or sugar snap peas, trimmed
- 1 yellow or white onion, sliced
- ⅓ cup olive oil
- Juice of 1 lemon
- 2 garlic cloves, minced
- Salt and pepper to taste
- ½ teaspoon oregano

In 1 inch of boiling water, steam fresh vegetables until crisp-tender: steam beans for 2 minutes, then add sweet peas, and after another minute add snow peas; cook another minute or two (green and yellow beans take 4 minutes, sweet peas 2 minutes, snow peas 1 minute). Rinse under cold running water. In large salad bowl, combine chickpeas, fresh vegetables, and sliced onion with olive oil, lemon juice, and garlic. Season with salt and pepper. Sprinkle with oregano. Toss and let stand for 30 minutes.

Serves 8.

Note: For a creamy dressing for dairy meals, mix equal parts plain yogurt and mayonnaise, then add minced garlic and salt and pepper to taste.

Mushroom Garlic Chicken

This family favorite is easy and delicious.

- 6 chicken breasts with skin and ribs or a 2- to 3-pound chicken cut into eighths
- ⅓ cup flour
- Salt to taste
- Pepper to taste
- 2 to 3 tablespoons olive oil
- 6 cloves garlic, peeled
- 12 ounces small or large mushrooms, cleaned (quarter large mushrooms)
- ⅓ cup balsamic vinegar
- 1 cup canned clear kosher chicken soup
- 1 large bay leaf
- ½ teaspoon dried thyme or 2 sprigs fresh thyme

Clean and dry chicken. Season flour with salt and pepper to taste. Dredge chicken breasts in flour mixture and shake off excess. Heat oil in heavy or non-stick skillet over medium heat. Sauté chicken, skin-side down, until brown on one side. Add garlic and mushrooms. Turn chicken and continue to cook until mushrooms are evenly cooked and chicken is brown on other side. Pour off any fat. Add vinegar, chicken soup, bay leaf, and thyme. Cover and simmer another 25 minutes.

Serves 6 to 8.

Poppy Seed Noodles.

Poppy Seed Noodles

- 1 12-ounce package medium egg noodles
- 3 tablespoons pareve margarine
- 3 or 4 tablespoons poppy seeds
- 2 teaspoons lemon juice
- 1 teaspoon salt
- Pepper to taste
- Chopped parsley

Prepare noodles according to package instructions. Drain and rinse. Toss with everything but parsley. Garnish with chopped parsley.

Serves 6 to 8.

Mushroom Garlic Chicken.

Snow Peas, Red Peppers, and Bamboo Shoots.

Snow Peas, Red Peppers, and Bamboo Shoots

- 2 pounds snow peas
- 2 tablespoons oil
- 1 8-ounce can slivered or sliced bamboo shoots, drained
- 1 red pepper, cut in ¼-inch strips
- ½ cup chicken-flavored broth
- 2 tablespoons soy sauce or tamari sauce
- 1 or 2 tablespoons dry sherry
- 1 tablespoon cornstarch
- 2 tablespoons water

Trim and remove strings from snow peas. Heat oil in wok or frying pan. Briefly stir-fry snow peas, bamboo shoots, and red peppers, about 1 to 2 minutes. Add broth, soy sauce, sherry, and cornstarch dissolved in water. Stir until thickened.

Serves 6 to 8.

Hamantaschen

The recipe for the hamantaschen dough came to me from Bea Kurtz of Livingston, New Jersey. It makes a particularly tender hamantasch. Try a variety of fillings.

Dough

- ¾ cup unsalted pareve margarine
- 1 cup sugar
- 1 egg
- ¼ cup orange juice
- 1½ teaspoons vanilla
- 3 cups flour
- 1 teaspoon baking soda
- ½ teaspoon salt

Cream margarine and sugar together until fluffy. Add egg and beat well. Stir in orange juice and vanilla and blend. Add flour, baking soda, and salt. Blend well. Chill 1 hour or more.

Preheat oven to 375 degrees F.

Roll on a floured board and cut into 3-inch rounds. Place 1 teaspoon of desired filling in the center of each round. Bring in sides and pinch sides hard to form a triangle. Bake on ungreased cookie sheet about 15 minutes.

Makes 3 dozen.

Hamantaschen.

Poppy Seed Filling I

- ½ to ¾ jar (9 ounces) poppy seed filling
- ¼ cup raisins
- ⅓ cup almonds, chopped
- Juice of half a lemon
- 1½ teaspoon grated lemon rind, or to taste

Combine ingredients.

Poppy Seed Filling II

- 1 cup ground poppy seed
- ¼ cup sugar
- 3 tablespoons light corn syrup
- 1 teaspoon vanilla or grated lemon peel
- ½ cup milk or water
- ⅓ cup raisins
- ½ cup chopped almonds (optional)

Combine ingredients and place in a saucepan on range. Simmer until thick, 5 to 10 minutes. Add more sugar if desired.

Damson Plum Filling

- ¾ jar (9 ounces) damson plum jam
- 3 tablespoons coconut
- 1 teaspoon lemon juice
- 1 teaspoon lemon rind
- ⅓ cup walnuts, chopped
- ¼ cup raisins
- 3 tablespoons apple, chopped (optional)

Combine ingredients and mix well.

Chocolate Filling

- 1 cup semisweet chocolate chips
- 2 tablespoons margarine
- 1 egg, beaten
- 1 teaspoon vanilla
- ⅓ cup sugar
- ½ cup toasted walnuts, chopped

Melt chocolate chips and margarine over low heat. Remove from heat and cool. Add egg, vanilla, sugar, and walnuts to chocolate and mix well.

Prune Filling

- 2 cups pitted steamed prunes
- ¼ cup sugar
- ½ cup raisins
- ½ cup walnuts or pecans, chopped
- Rind of 1 orange
- Rind of 1 lemon
- Juice of 1 lemon

In food processor, process prunes until smooth. Place prunes in bowl with the rest of the ingredients. Mix well.

Ma'amoul

These Middle Eastern pastries are popular in Israel around Purim. They have a pielike dough and are filled with ground or finely chopped nuts and sugar.

Pastry
- 2 cups sifted flour (flour should be sifted before measuring)
- 1¼ sticks pareve margarine
- Approximately 3 to 4 tablespoons water (or use 2 to 3 teaspoons rose water, available at specialty and health food stores, and the rest tap water, if desired)

Filling
- ½ cup coarsely ground almonds or walnuts
- 3 tablespoons sugar
- 1 teaspoon cinnamon or rose water

Preheat oven to 350 degrees F. Put flour and margarine in food processor and process until crumblike. Add water until soft dough forms. Cover for a half hour.

Combine filling ingredients.

Form dough into small walnut-size balls. Make hole in center with thumb. Fill with heaping teaspoon of nut filling. Press sides together to close the dough. Form into balls. Make a design on top with fork tines. Place on ungreased cookie sheets. Bake 25 to 30 minutes. When cool, roll in confectioners' sugar.

Makes about 20 cookies.

Cranberry Fruit Punch

Using juice concentrates and an ice ring prevents the fruit punch from becoming too diluted.

- 1 12-ounce can frozen cranberry-cherry, cranberry-raspberry, or cranberry juice concentrate
- 1 6-ounce can frozen pineapple or pineapple-orange juice concentrate
- 1½ cups orange juice
- ¼ cup lemon or lime juice
- 3 cups ice-cold water
- 1 liter bottle chilled ginger ale
- ½ cup light rum (optional)
- ¼ cup orange liqueur (Triple Sec, Cointreau, or Grand Marnier) (optional)

Make an ice ring mold if desired by freezing 1 inch of water in a ring mold. Add some mint leaves, orange and lemon or lime slices, and pineapple wedges, and top with ½ inch of water. Freeze until firm. Fill mold with more water until mold is ¾ full. Freeze until firm.

In a punch bowl, mix cranberry juice concentrate, pineapple juice concentrate, orange juice, lemon or lime juice, and cold water. Stir. Carefully add chilled ginger ale just before serving so it will fizz. Unmold ice ring by wrapping with hot towel and inverting onto plate. Place on top of punch. To spike punch, add light rum and orange liqueur.

Serves 8.

CHAPTER SIX

PASSOVER

xactly one Hebrew calendar month separates Purim from Passover, the most important and oldest of the Jewish festivals, and, for many, the climax of the Jewish festival year.

Passover (*Hag Hapesah* in Hebrew), which begins at sundown on the fourteenth day of Nisan (the fifteenth of Nisan), is a seven-day holiday for Reform Jews and Jews in Israel, while traditional Jews in the Diaspora commemorate Passover for eight days. The first two and the last two days of Passover in the Diaspora are holidays when no work is done; the middle, or intermediate, days are semiholidays known as *Hol Hamoed*.

THE BIRTH OF THE JEWISH PEOPLE

Passover marks the dawn of Jewish nationhood, Israel's birth as a people. The Passover story predates Purim by thousands of years, but the Purim story as a metaphor for anti-Semitism was only possible because of Passover, when the Jewish people were transformed from bands of lowly Hebrew slaves into a separate and distinct Israelite nation.

The Passover story as told in the Book of Exodus begins with the death of Joseph and the rise of a new Egyptian Pharaoh, widely thought to be Ramses II, and, later, his son Merneptah. This new Egyptian leader enslaves the Hebrews. According to biblical commentaries, the cruel practices that were forced on the Jews included the separation of husbands and wives and a preposterously high daily quota of mortar and bricks required of each Israelite slave. The constant indignities and oppression robbed the slaves of their humanity and often their lives.

Opposite: This is a lavishly illustrated page from a medieval German Haggadah. Above: "And the Egyptians treated us harshly and oppressed us, and imposed hard labor on us" (Deut. 26:6, quoted in the Haggadah).

THE STORY OF THE EXODUS

When Pharaoh orders all newborn Hebrew males to be killed, one woman hides her child among the reeds of the Nile river. The infant is found and named Moses by Pharaoh's daughter and is raised in Pharaoh's court. When Moses reaches young adulthood, he visits his enslaved kinsmen and is mysteriously drawn to them. Witnessing his people's brutalization, Moses comes to their defense and even kills an Egyptian taskmaster who is beating a Hebrew slave. At a Divine mystical encounter at a burning bush, Moses is called upon by God to become the leader of his people, to go to Pharaoh and ask him to let his people go. Pharaoh is recalcitrant, despite plague after terrible plague. Only after the Egyptian first-born are struck down, and the households of the Hebrews, whose doorposts are marked with lambs' blood, are passed over (hence the name Passover) does Pharaoh relent. As soon as the Israelites leave, however, the Egyptians follow in hot pursuit. The Hebrews cross the Red Sea (literally the Sea of Reeds) on dry land when it parts, but their Egyptian pursuers drown as the walls of the sea come crashing down upon them. Known as the Exodus from Egypt, this event is what the Passover holiday commemorates.

The Exodus was one of the defining moments in ancient Jewish history, and is recalled time and again in the Jewish liturgy, which is replete with references to the God of Israel who took the children of Israel out of Egyptian bondage to make them a people. So bitter was the memory of servitude, and so sweet the taste of freedom that the Exodus etched itself permanently into the Jewish psyche and has become the paradigm of the Jewish experience.

Some critical scholars speculate that Passover's roots actually predate the Exodus, and that two distinct holidays were originally observed: one of nomadic or seminomadic shepherds, and one of farmers. The older of the two, Pesah, the holiday of the shepherds, was celebrated in the spring by slaughtering a sheep or goat, smearing its blood on tent posts, and hastily eating the meal of roasted meat in family groups. The later pastoral festival, the feast of unleavened bread, was also celebrated in the spring in honor of the barley harvest. Before the harvest, the ancient Israelite peasants who tilled the land would rid their homes of the previous year's leaven or sourdough, and eat unleavened bread. According to this point of view, both holidays eventually merged into one, became associated with the Passover story in the Bible, and were given a historical reinterpretation. Scholars have proposed other theories about the origins of the Passover holiday as well.

PASSOVER AS A PILGRIMAGE FESTIVAL

By Temple times, the importance of Passover was undisputed, and Passover gained the prominence it was to retain. Marking the beginning of the barley harvest, Passover was one of three agricultural pilgrimage holidays, along with Shavuot and Sukkot. It was grandly celebrated with pomp and ceremonial sacrifices at the Temple in Jerusalem. The paschal lambs (Pesah sacrifice) were later roasted and eaten in large group gatherings. Always occurring in the springtime, and known also as *Hag Haaviv*, the holiday of spring, it was a time of natural beauty and rebirth, of new possibilities and new beginnings. Falling on the first month of the Hebrew calendar, Passover once headed the Jewish calendar year.

The reason for Passover's continuing appeal—long after its agricultural origins receded in importance with the destruction of the Second Temple and many Jews living in the Diaspora—

BONDAGE IN EGYPT

A change in the relations of the Egyptians towards the Israelites had, indeed, been noticeable immediately after the death of Joseph, but they did not throw off their mask completely until Levi, the last of the sons of Jacob, was no more. Then the slavery of the Israelites supervened in good earnest.

The first hostile act on the part of the Egyptians was to deprive the Israelites of their fields, their vineyards, and the gifts that Joseph had sent to his brethren. Not content with these hostile acts, they sought to do them harm in other ways.

The physical strength and heroism of the Israelites were extraordinary and therefore alarming to the Egyptians. There were many occasions at that time for the display of prowess. Not long after the death of Levi occurred that of the Egyptian king Magron, who had been brought up by Joseph, and therefore was not wholly without grateful recollection of what he and his family had accomplished for the welfare of Egypt. But his son and successor Malol, together with his whole court, knew not the sons of Jacob and their achievements, and they did not scruple to oppress the Hebrews.

The final breach between them and the Egyptians took place during the wars waged by Malol against Zepho, the grandson of Esau. In the course of it, the Israelites had saved the Egyptians from a crushing defeat, but instead of being grateful they sought only the undoing of their benefactors, from fear that the great strength of the Hebrews might be turned against them.

Even as a bird is held fast in the hand of the hunter who, if he wishes, slays it, or if he wishes, lets it live, so Israel was held fast in the hand of the Egyptians, as Scripture notes in saying (Ex. 3.8), *I am come down to deliver them out of the hand of the Egyptians (Midrash Tehillim* 107.4).

From the *Midrash*.

The search for hametz, Bedikat Hametz, *takes place on the evening before Passover. This engraving shows a mother hiding pieces of leavened bread in places where they can be found.*

was a new emphasis on Passover as a national and historical holiday of freedom. Another name for Passover was *zeman heiruteinu,* the time of our liberation. Passover's universal message of hope and deliverance was that freedom was attainable despite persecution; liberty was a basic human right; and the dignity of every human being was sacred. The architect of that concept of freedom was seen as God Himself, the protector of the oppressed, who had rescued His own people.

To comprehend and transmit this concept of freedom required thought and preparation. As a result, Passover evolved into the most complex and elaborate of the Jewish festivals. It is a holiday with its own rules, rituals, and foods.

PREPARATION FOR PASSOVER

The countdown to Passover begins right after Purim. During the months before Passover, the traditional Jewish house is cleansed of all *hametz* (grain products and their derivatives) and is ideally spring-cleaned, as well. The whole household undergoes a transformation. The old and familiar are temporarily discarded to create a sense of renewal and newness. Pots and pans, dishes, and utensils specifically set aside for use on Passover help alter the Jewish home. Certain utensils, glasses, and flatware can be made kosher for Passover through a cleansing process called *kashering,* which involves immersion or purging, depending on what the item is made of and how it was used.

HAMETZ: THE ULTIMATE CONTAMINANT

Eight days out of the year, foods that may be consumed without thought as to their kashrut (ritual fitness) suddenly become forbidden. And just as suddenly, when eight days of Passover have concluded, these same foods are permitted once again! Herein lies a mystery and an opportunity for interpretation. The forbidden foods that fall under the category of *hametz* (usually translated as "leavened bread") generally include, but are not limited to: all consumables that are prepared using the five species of grain—wheat, barley, oats, spelt, and rye—that have been allowed to leaven, rise, or ferment, such as cakes, cereals, crackers, and alcohol, to name just a few. Even accidental admixtures of the smallest quantity of *hametz* make any food forbidden to eat on Passover. Owning, buying, or selling such food is equally prohibited, and traditional Jewish households go to great lengths to rid their homes of *hametz.*

Rabbi David Ben Solomon Ibn Abi Zimra (1479–1573) wondered why the sages were so extraordinarily stringent when it came to *hametz.* Foods prohibited by the Torah were, of course, forbidden, but a certain leniency marked the rabbinic attitude. Why were the Rabbis so strict with *hametz?*

The reason, mused Rabbi David Ben Solomon, was that *hametz* could be considered a symbol of evil in the world and of the evil inclination within a human being, and that just as it was important to rid the house of *hametz* during Passover, so it was important for all humanity to rid the world of evil. And, of course, even the most insignificant presence of evil has the power to contaminate.

Rabbi David Ben Solomon was not the first to suggest that *hametz* was a powerful metaphor. In the Talmud (Berachot 17a), yeast in dough is compared to corruption, to the evil inclination that rises and ferments in the heart. And Philo, the Alexandrian philosopher and commentator (c. 20 B.C.E.–50 C.E.), also uses the presence of *hametz* to represent the presence of evil.

Other rabbis further developed the idea of *hametz* to refer to pride, arrogance, and vanity, all of which puff up the ego as yeast leavens dough. Idolatry, which supplants the worship of God, is also a kind of *hametz,* or leavening, because the deification of anything created by human beings ultimately corrupts and eclipses the spiritual link between God and His creation.

And so what begins as the cleansing of a home for the observance of Passover from all that is leavened is transformed into a spiritual cleansing as well.

This ritual ridding the home of *hametz* can also be a contemporary symbol of Passover. Human oppression, prejudice, and persecution is the ultimate *hametz* between human beings and, in a civilized society, should be unacceptable and intolerable. Even the slightest admixture of *hametz* contaminates the whole; human freedom and dignity must never be compromised.

HOW TO MAKE A KITCHEN
KOSHER FOR PASSOVER

It takes several days of hard work to prepare a kitchen for Passover, but a spotless, gleaming kitchen is a must. Do not hesitate to hire extra cleaning help if you can. Here are some tips for those who change over their homes for Passover.

1. Clean insides of cabinets of all crumbs.
2. Reline cabinets, especially those cleared of *hametz*, where kosher-for-Passover food, dishes, or utensils will go.
3. Place *hametz* items in boxes to be stored away, and use up half-eaten boxes of *hametz* in the month before Passover.
4. Clean out the refrigerator, and if necessary, defrost the freezer. Clean thoroughly, including the gaskets where *hametz* can accumulate. Store *hametz* items in another refrigerator or give to a neighbor for safekeeping. Some people line their refrigerators with aluminum foil for Passover.
5. Clean the range thoroughly including the area under burners. Use the self-clean cycle if you have one, or chemical oven cleaners if you don't. For a continuous-cleaning oven, clean as for a regular oven. Do not forget the oven racks. Do not use for twenty-four hours. Turn burners on highest heat for at least fifteen minutes (five to ten minutes for electric burners) and turn the regular oven on the highest heat, including the broiler, for a half hour. Some people keep the heat on longer—a half hour to an hour for burners, and an hour or more for the oven.
6. For a microwave, clean thoroughly and do not use for twenty-four hours. Place a cup of water inside, and turn the microwave on until it is completely steamed or the water disappears.
7. Clean the sink thoroughly. Pour boiling water over all sinks, and use plastic basins in porcelain sinks.
8. Dishwashers are tricky. Some authorities permit their use after they have been thoroughly cleaned and not used for twenty-four hours and then operated on a full cycle with detergent. Others insist on new racks. Others do not permit their use if they have porcelain interiors.
9. Scrub down and cover the countertops. A good covering is lightly adhesive shelf paper that sticks and is washable, but comes off easily without leaving a residue. Vinyl or plastic coverings or aluminum foil can also be used. Leave one small counter area free for *hametz*, which can be quickly covered in the morning before the first seder.
10. Clean the table and chairs, taking care to clean in the cracks of a table that opens and the recesses of the chairs, and cover the table with plastic.
11. Tape shut or tie with a cord or rubber bands any cabinets that are not for Passover use.
12. *Kasher* utensils that may be made kosher for Passover according to rabbinical advice.

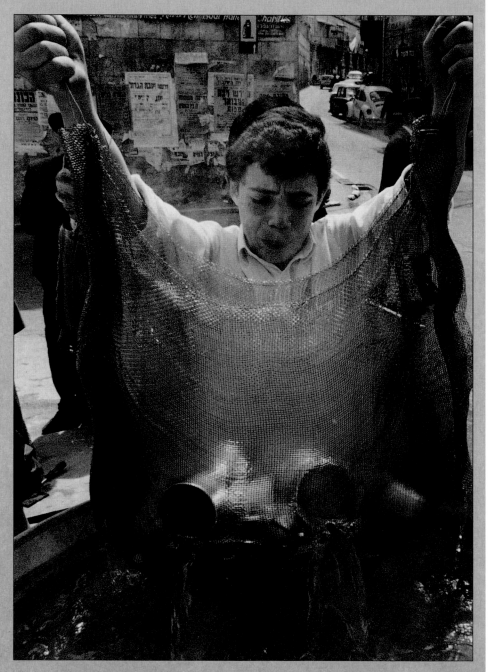

An ultra-Orthodox boy in the Mea Shearim neighborhood of Jerusalem grimaces while making utensils kosher for Passover by lowering them into scalding water.

Foods containing leavening of any kind, such as bread and flour products, are forbidden. Only specifically designated "kosher-for-Passover" foods are to be used (except for fruits, vegetables, and a few other natural products). The best-known of the Passover foods is matzah. A flat wafer or cracker made only of flour and water and containing no leavening, matzah is mixed and placed in the oven for no more than eighteen minutes. According to tradition, matzah is the bread of Passover because the fleeing Hebrews had no time to make bread, and baked matzah instead. It was also the bread of the desert. Matzah, therefore, became the symbol of the bread of affliction as well as the food of freedom.

In addition to the physical preparations, there are also many intellectual and spiritual preparations for Passover. To experience the holiday fully requires time, thought, and effort. One is enjoined in the Bible to retell the Passover story from generation to generation so that its message remains forever fresh and compelling. "And you shall explain to your child on that day, it is because of what the Lord did for me when I went free from Egypt" (Exod. 13:8). The core ritual on Passover, and one that is observed by more Jews than any other ritual in the Jewish holiday calendar, is the Passover seder, which is more than a warm family get-together; it is high drama experienced in an elaborate set of rituals engaging both mind and heart, intellect and soul. The guidebook and text for this home ritual is the Haggadah, which means "the telling."

Familiarizing oneself with the Haggadah and its commentaries before the seder enhances the Passover experience. Lively, in-depth, and stimulating discussion of the Haggadah was especially encouraged by the Rabbis years ago, when they added their own interpretation to the Haggadah by equating the strong arm of Rome, under which they lived, with the yoke of the Egyptians. Ideally this kind of creative interpretation should be the focus of the Passover seder. It lends excitement to the seder and gives it a magical quality. It makes the past part of the present by engaging each participant and making Passover not just the story of one's ancestors but one's own as well. This ancient holiday retains a youthfulness of spirit with its questions, reinterpretations, expansions, and additions. It is a holiday of springtime, hope, renewal, the sprouting of new ideas, and the flowering of the human intellect and spirit.

THE HAGGADAH: A BOOK FOR ALL GENERATIONS

No book in Jewish life is as beloved as the Haggadah. Other sacred books in the Jewish library, from the Torah to the *siddur*, from Talmud to Responsa literature, are pored over with care. No marks are deliberately made; the margins are clean, and the pages are turned with a gentle hand.

But a Haggadah is stamped by last year's spilled wine, by matzah crumbs that cling to the binding, by the stains of fingers past, and fragrances of other Passover seders filled with songs and conversations emanating from the old and venerated text. The Haggadah is script and folk songs, history and myth, interesting culinary delights, and sacred text. More than just a creation of the Rabbis, it is a book of the folk and for the folk; a book for children, and also for the wise and learned. Though it is a book for one season and one holiday, it is really for all generations.

The Haggadah has had thousands of editions. It was the earliest to be painstakingly illustrated, and there are a few manuscripts of breathtaking beauty that are housed in libraries and private collections. Some authorities say that the first printed Haggadah was created in Guadalajara, Spain, in 1482. Since then, there has been a proliferation of Haggadot. The text has remained the same for the most part, but there are various creative illustrations and typographies, which make the study of Haggadot a visually stimulating and enriching experience.

The theme of oppression and redemption, of slavery followed by liberation is so appealing that many recently published Haggadot tie contemporary events and concerns into the ancient mosaic of the Haggadah. For example, it is not unusual for African-Americans and Jews to sit and weave together in a single text the story of their respective enslavement and the hope for universal emancipation and freedom. When Russian Jews were still in "bondage" in the Soviet Union and demanded that the Communist government let them go, many prayers and some new editions of the Haggadah were published to share the cry for liberation of the Russian Jews. Some Haggadot published in the late 1960s and early 1970s reflected the anti–Vietnam War movement, and other Haggadot blended the women's rights movement with the search for equality and dignity.

In modern Israel, some Haggadot tell the story of the creation of the state along with the story of the ancient liberation from Egypt. Others contain the grim story of the Holocaust, and the people who managed to survive intertwine their story with that of Egyptian oppression.

Some Haggadot were used a while and then disappeared. But some of the modern additional texts found their way into the traditional Haggadah and will most probably remain as part of the dynamic and growing literature. Many modern traditional Haggadot now have a prayer for those people lost during the Holocaust. Just after the meal is concluded, and just as the cup of Elijah is filled, a special prayer is recited in memory of the six million, followed by the tune "Ani Ma'amin" hoping for the coming of the Messianic era.

Another addition in some modern Haggadot is an actual fifth cup of wine celebrating the miracle of the reestablishment of the modern state of Israel. A special prayer of gratitude is recited, and the fifth cup is consumed in the hope that Israel will always be a country dedicated to justice and truth. The Haggadah, with its wine stains and its fingerprints from the past, is a treasured national family album of unusual power and beauty. As families and guests gather around a table prepared for the seder, and as the Haggadah is opened for song and recitation, conversation and meditation, history comes alive vividly and graphically, teaching yet another generation the story of the Exodus from Egypt and its eternal meaning and message.

THE PASSOVER TABLE

The Passover seder table is beautifully set with seasonal flowers and Passover finery: a lovely tablecloth; sparkling candlesticks; wine cups for everyone, with a large goblet in the center for Elijah; a wine decanter filled with kosher wine; bowls of salt water for dipping, symbolic of the tears shed by the Israelite slaves; and three matzot, one atop the other in a special layered cover or on a tiered plate symbolizing three categories of Jews—Kohen (Priest), Levite, and Israelite. Just as the three matzot are equally important, so are all Jews that make up the household of Israel. The centerpiece of the table is the *kearah*, the seder plate. Symbolic foods are eaten or pointed to during the course of the seder. The symbolic foods are: 1) *haroset*, which symbolizes the mortar that the enslaved Hebrews used for building purposes. A finely chopped mixture of apples, nuts, cinnamon, honey, and wine is popular among Ashkenazic Jews, while the use of dried fruit and spices is more common among Sephardic Jews; 2) *karpas*, which is a symbol of spring. It can be any green vegetable—such as parsley, celery, or even baby artichokes (or a cooked potato); 3) *z'roa*, the paschal sacrifice, symbolized by a roasted lamb shank bone, poultry neck, or a boiled or roasted beet for vegetarians; 4) *beitzah*, a roasted egg, the symbol of the *hagigah* or regular festival sacrifice; 5) *maror*, or bitter herbs. A horseradish root, slivered or grated, or a bitter lettuce such as romaine or escarole, symbolic of the bitterness of slavery, can be used. On some seder plates there is also *hazeret*—additional maror for the korekh sandwich.

Seder Plate Arrangement

Beitzah   Z'roa

Maror

Karpas   Haroset

(Hazeret)

A Passover seder plate with the symbolic Passover foods.

THE SEDER

The word "seder" means "order," and there is a definite order to the Passover home service, which begins soon after sundown. Each person should have his or her own Haggadah; Haggadot with commentaries are especially welcome to stimulate further discussion. Uniform Haggadot make the seder easier to follow and encourage participation. Everyone is invited to participate in the seder, and parts of the Haggadah are often meted out. Each seder is unique because each person brings to it his or her own experiences, insights, and family traditions. Many family traditions and melodies have grown at the seder, where often new traditions are spontaneously created and then perpetuated, making each seder a fresh experience. Children are very much a part of the evening's festivities, which they enliven with their comments, antics, and singing. Much of the seder is deliberately designed to hold their interest.

The seder begins with *kadesh*—the recitation of the Passover kiddush. This toast sanctifies the holiday with a blessing over wine, the most aristocratic of drinks and one that is mentioned in the Bible. Most Jewish festivals and Shabbat begin with the kiddush. At the seder kiddush, the first of four glasses of wine is drunk in honor of the four biblical expressions of redemption. A fifth glass, in dispute, becomes the cup of Elijah. The cup is in dispute because there is a fifth expression of redemption: "I will bring you into your land." Some Rabbis felt that this called for a fifth cup of wine, but others disagreed. The issue was left for Elijah to resolve. In some seders another cup is drunk at the end of the seder in gratitude for the state of Israel (see page 87). At one point during the seder, drops of wine are spilled on one's plate in memory of the ten plagues visited upon the Egyptians, to show that one's joy cannot be complete when others had to suffer. We should not gloat over the downfall of our enemies. Even the Talmud says that when the Egyptians were drowning, the heavenly angels wanted to sing, but God stopped them and

MAH NISHTANAH*

Ma nish-ta -na ha - lai - la ha - zeh mi - kol__ha - lei - lot mi-kol__ ha - lei - lot she - b' - chol ha - lei - lot a - nu och - lin cha metz__ u - ma - tza cha - metz__ u - ma - tza ha - lai - la ha -zeh ha - lai la ha - zeh ku - lo__ ma - tza__

Why is this night different than all other nights of the year?
On all the nights of the year we eat both bread and matza, but on the night of Passover we eat only matza.

*See music on page 118.

A Passover seder in New York City in the 1890s.

admonished, "The works of My hands are drowning in the sea. How can you want to sing?"

Next is *Urhatz*, the ritual washing of the hands, without blessing. It was customary to wash one's hands before dipping, which follows. It is also done to remove ritual impurity that can be imparted by something moist, such as the dipping of the vegetable into water. This serves as a reminder of Temple times when people had to be cautious about transmitting ritual impurity from hand to hand, and therefore person to person.

Karpas: the eating of the vegetable dipped in salt water, symbolic of springtime. This is done with a blessing over "the fruit of the earth." It is intended to arouse children's curiosity.

Yahatz: the splitting of the middle matzah, the larger part of which is set aside as the *afikoman*. The *afikoman* (the word comes from Greek) is the "dessert of the seder." It is customary for children to hide or to look for the *afikoman*, depending on one's tradition.

Magid: this is the core experience of the seder, the retelling of the Passover story. The Mishnah says that each generation must see itself as if it personally came out of Egypt. This is the essence of the seder—to re-create the experience of slavery and freedom through rituals, foods, prayer, reenactment, dynamic exchange, and lively discussion. This allows each ensuing generation of Jews to reclaim the Passover holiday as its own. For that reason, the seder begins with the four questions, usually asked by the youngest family member. The purpose of questions such as "Why is this night different?" or "Why

DAYEINU*

Rhythmically   **Folk Song**

I - lu ho-tsi, ho - tsi - a - nu, ho - tsi - a - nu mi - mits-ra - yim

ho - tsi - a - nu mi - mits-ra - yim, da - yei - nu. I - lu ho - tsi

ho-tsi-a - nu, ho-tsi-a-nu mi-mits-ra-yim, ho-tsi-a - nu mi-mits-ra-

yim da - yei - nu. Da - da - yei-nu___ da - da - yei-nu,___ da - da

- yei- nu, da - da - yei-nu, da - da - yei-nu, da-yei - nu. yei - nu, da - yei-nu

I-lu na-tan la-nu et ha-Sha-bat, da-yei-nu.
I-lu na-tan la-nu et ha-To-rah, da-yei-nu.
I-lu hih-ni-sa-nu l'E-rets Yis-ra-el, da-yei-nu.

Had He done nothing more than take us out of Egypt
    dayeinu (for that alone we should have been grateful).
 Had he given us the Sabbath and nothing more,
    dayeinu.
Had He given us the Torah and nothing more, dayeinu.
Had He brought us into the land of Israel, dayeinu.

From *The Songs We Sing*, edited by Harry Coopersmith.
© 1950 United Synagogue of America. Used with permission.

*See music on page 118.

L'SHANAH HABA'AH[*]

L'- sha - na ha - ba - a bi - ru-sha-la - yim l'- sha-na ha - ba - a bi-ru - sha - la - yim l'- sha - na ha - ba - a bi - ru - sha - la - yim l'- sha - na ha - ba - a bi - ru - sha - la - yim hab' - nu - ya la la la la la la.....................la........................la........................la

L'sha-na ha-ba-a bi-ru-sha-ly-yim hab'nu-ya

Next year in the rebuilt Jerusalem.

*See music on page 118.

ELIJAH: PROPHET AND SYMBOL

No prophet in Jewish history and legend has attained as much mythical stature as Elijah. In legend and parable, Elijah becomes a protective presence at every boy's circumcision; stands solicitously at the bed of a dying person; is present at the conclusion of the Sabbath as the *Havdalah* candle is extinguished; roams the world touching the daily lives of the common folk by disguising himself as an ordinary human being; will one day be called up to announce the coming of the Messianic age according to the prophet Malachi (3:23); and, during the Passover seder, is welcomed through a door that is opened for him in the hopes that he indeed has arrived to usher in an age of peace and tranquillity for all humanity. Elijah is present during critical, transitional periods in the lives of individuals and the destiny of the Jewish nation.

But in life, Elijah was often an unforgiving prophet of harsh judgment, fire, and brimstone. As described in the First and Second Book of Kings, Elijah is irascible and austere. His denunciation of Ahab, the weak and faithless king of Israel, and his verbal attacks and eventual execution of the false prophets who encouraged idolatrous practices, prompted by the wicked queen Jezebel, are accompanied by an equally harsh judgment against himself; he thought he had failed at transforming Israelite society into a God-fearing and spiritual people. Yet, as a symbol, he is transformed into a compassionate and helpful presence, the companion of the ill and the depressed, the guardian of the poor, the champion of the ordinary human being, and the harbinger of the Messianic age.

The presence of the prophet Elijah is especially felt during Passover. Immediately after the seder meal, a fifth cup of wine is poured, called the cup of Elijah. The door is opened, as though to welcome in the prophet, and a mystical presence seems to enter the home, benign and full of promise. It is almost as though the austere prophet wants to come back as the compassionate and kindly personage he could never fully be in life.

With true genius and imagination, rabbinic legend and folklore created an Elijah who liberated his own personality, teaching us that any liberation, any Messianic age, must begin with love for humankind before real freedom can be exercised. Thus, Elijah, the austere and unforgiving prophet in life, becomes in legend a compassionate and caring person.

do we dip twice instead of once?" is to stimulate discussion even though some of the questions are never directly answered. Within the *magid* section are biblical quotations followed by rabbinic commentaries and thoughtful and sometimes humorous and exaggerated observations, as well as historical anecdotes and folktales.

Rahtzah: each participant washes his or her hands with a blessing, as is normally done before eating bread. Often, while the leader is engaged in this activity, the *afikoman* mysteriously disappears.

Motzi Matzah: the ritual eating of the matzah. First, the usual blessing over bread is said, and then another is said for the matzah. The matzot that are eaten are pieces from the top and middle matzot.

Maror: the eating of the bitter herbs together with the haroset, which sweetens the bitter taste. Another interpretation is that the Hebrew word *mar* can mean "teacher" as well as "bitter"; one can learn from bitter experiences.

Korekh: the eating of the *maror* and the matzah together in sandwich form as prescribed by the first-century sage Hillel. The bottom matzah is used for this.

Shulhan Orekh: the festive and elaborate Passover banquet is an integral part of the seder and comes between the two parts of the *Hallel* to emphasize this point. Unlike ancient Greek and Roman banquets, where orgies and revelry after meals were common, the seder has an authentic Jewish stamp of sanctity.

The meal ends with *Tzafun:* the retrieval and ransoming of the hidden *afikoman* by parents and children. Without it, the seder cannot proceed. The *afikoman* is symbolic of the paschal lamb, the last food in the mouths of our forebears. The taste of matzah should be the last taste of food for the evening. In some Sephardic communities, it was customary to keep pieces of the *afikoman* as a good-luck charm.

Barekh: the Grace after Meals is next, followed by the third cup of wine.

The cup of Elijah is then filled and the front door is opened to welcome Elijah, who symbolizes future redemption. Some think that the opening of the door was to show no fear on this biblical night of watching, known as *leil shimurim*. This is the time the Holocaust is often recalled, and new sections have been added to some Haggadot in memory of the six million murdered Jews and the Warsaw Ghetto uprising, which took place on the second night of Passover.

In contrast to the seriousness of the first part, the rest of the seder is made up of the rousing songs of praise of the *Hallel*, the drinking of the fourth cup of wine, and a medley of lively folk songs, a medieval addition. These songs are designed to keep the children awake and entertained. The singing is an expression of true inner freedom, which is attained by having gone through the entire process of the seder and its evocation of slavery. The end of the seder, *Nirtzah* (which in most Haggadot comes before the songs), is marked by the spirited recitation of "Next year in Jerusalem!" (or "Next year in the rebuilt Jerusalem," if you are in Israel) symbolic not only of Jerusalem physically, but of a spiritual Jerusalem of peace, justice, harmony, and freedom.

Young and old, family and friends participate in the Passover seder. The seder is now the most observed and beloved Jewish home ritual.

THE MEANING OF PASSOVER

The Passover holiday perhaps best symbolizes what all Jewish festivals are about: home and children, family and friends, traditions and food, songs and laughter, values and teachings. More than any other ritual, the seder is a microcosm of the Jewish experience, for it evokes both the bitterness and sweetness of Jewish life through the ages. It is a timely reminder of the tortuous journey from slavery to freedom. Passover is a holiday when Jews reach out to one another and open their doors to strangers and the less fortunate. It is also a time for Jews to empathize with others, to open their hearts to the pain and suffering of other people. It is a time when Jews remind themselves that whenever anyone is enslaved anywhere in the world, no one is really free, and that each person has a responsibility to work that much harder for the redemption and freedom of every human being. For the Jew, the Exodus is both the memory and the promise of that freedom.

TRADITIONS AND CUSTOMS ASSOCIATED WITH PASSOVER

- Funds for the poor called *maot hittim* are collected by the community before Passover to buy food for the indigent.
- The Sabbath before Passover is known as *Shabbat Hagadol*, or the Great Sabbath. In Eastern Europe, this was one of the two times during the year that the rabbi would sermonize (the other occasion was Shabbat Shuvah between Rosh Hashanah

CHAD GADYA*

Allegretto   **Traditional**

Chad gad - ya _____ chad gad - ya chad gad - ya _____ chad
gad - ya d' - za - bin a - ba bi - trei zu - zei chad gad ya_____
chad gad - ya v'a a - ta shun - ra v' - ach - la l'gad - ya d' - za - bin a -
ba bi - trei _____ zu - zei chad gad - ya _____ chad gad - ya

My father bought an only kid for two zuzim. A cat came and ate the kid; a dog came and bit the cat; an only kid, an only kid.

*See music on page 119.

and Yom Kippur). It is customary among some Jews to study the Haggadah in the afternoon of *Shabbat Hagadol* until the end of the song *Dayenu*.

- The Fast of the Firstborn (*Taanit Bekhorim*) is a minor fast day beginning on the morning before Passover to commemorate firstborn Hebrew sons who were spared in Egypt during the tenth plague. The fast begins at sunrise, but can be abrogated by a *siyyum*, in which studying and completing the last passage of a Talmudic tractate is followed by a religious meal, *seudah shel mitzvah*, which ends the fast.
- *Mekhirat hametz*—the selling of *hametz*. One is not allowed to own hametz during Passover. The Rabbis created a legal method by which one's *hametz* is sold to a non-Jew for Passover and bought back after the end of the holiday. This is done through a bill of sale with the rabbi acting as an agent.
- *Bedikat hametz*—Inspecting for *hametz* is a charming family ceremony conducted the night before Passover to hunt for the last remains of *hametz*. Pieces of bread are deliberately hidden in specific areas and then searched for with candle, feather, and spoon.

The candle, often held by a child, is used to light one's way around the house. The feather is used to brush the *hametz* into a spoon and from there into a paper napkin, bag, or plate. There is a special blessing recited before the search for *hametz*.

Barukh Atah Adonai Eloheinu melekh haolam asher kideshanu b'mitzvotav v'tzivanu al biur hametz.

(Blessed are You, O Lord our God, ruler of the universe, who has sanctified us with His commandments and commanded us to remove all *hametz*.)

Bittul hametz—a special formula is recited after the search to nullify ownership of *hametz*.

"All leaven in my possession that I have not seen or removed of which I am unaware is hereby nullified and rendered ownerless as the dust of the earth."

Biur hametz—The *hametz* that was collected the night before is taken outdoors and burned, and the nullification formula is repeated.

TAL

By Eleazar Kalir (sixth or seventh century Palestinian Hebrew poet); translated by Israel Zangwill.

Dew, precious dew, unto Your land forlorn,
Pour out our blessing in Your exultation,
To strengthen us with ample wine and corn,
And give Your chosen city safe foundation
  In dew.

Dew, precious dew, the good year's crown, we wait,
That earth in pride and glory may be fruited,
And that the city once so desolate
Into a gleaming crown may be transmuted
  By dew.

Dew, precious dew, let fall upon the land;
From heaven's treasury be this accorded;
So shall the darkness by a beam be spanned,
The faithful of Your vineyard be rewarded
  With dew.

Dew, precious dew, to make the mountains sweet,
The savor of Your excellence recalling.
Deliver us from exile, we entreat,
So we may sing Your praises, softly falling
  As dew.

Dew, precious dew, our granaries to fill,
And us with youthful freshness to enharden.
Beloved God, uplift us at Your will
And make us as a richly watered garden
  With dew.

Dew, precious dew, that we are harvest reap,
And guard our fatted flocks and herds from leanness.
Behold our people follows You like sheep,
And looks to You to give the earth her greenness
  With dew.

Reprinted from *Siddur Sim Shalom*, edited by Rabbi Jules Harlow. © 1985 by the Rabbinical Assembly. Reprinted with permission of the Rabbinical Assembly.

- Ashkenazic Jews do not eat *kitniyot* on Passover (rice, millet, peas, beans, corn, and lentils) because these foods can be ground into flour and can appear like *hametz*. Mustard, sesame, and sunflower seeds are also considered *kitniyot*. Sephardic Jews do not have this tradition.

- Reclining on a pillow to the left at the seder, particularly when eating matzah. In the ancient world reclining was a sign of being free. The leader or each participant can recline on pillows, depending on one's custom. The seder is full of ancient Greek and Roman customs that have been adapted and Judaized.

- In some traditional homes, the leader of the seder will wear a *kittel*, a white garment used on festive occasions. Some bridegrooms wear a *kittel* at their wedding, signifying a state of purity and joy.

- There is a custom among some Jews not to eat matzah from Purim until the night of the first seder, so the taste of matzah will be fresh. The obligation to eat matzah is only for the first night of Passover. It is optional for the rest of the holiday, when the injunction is only not to eat *hametz*. *Matzah shmurah* is often used at the seder. These are usually handmade round matzot made from wheat that is watched from the time of reaping through baking to ensure that it does not come in contact with water.

- Serving hard-boiled eggs just before the meal, as an appetizer, which neutralizes the taste of *maror*. Eggs are also a sign of fertility, birth, death, and renewal. There is a saying that the more Jews are oppressed, the stronger they become—like hard-boiled eggs, which become harder the longer they are cooked. The egg was also served as an hors d'oeuvre in the ancient world.

- On the second night of Passover, the counting of the omer begins, which continues for forty-nine days until Shavuot. The omer (a measure of grain) was in commemoration of the sheaves of barley brought to the Temple in gratitude for the harvest.

- Reading from the Song of Songs, *Shir Hashirim*, on the intermediate Shabbat of Pesah or the last day of Pesah if it falls on Shabbat. The Song of Songs was seen by the Rabbis as a love song between God and Israel which was appropriate to the theme of Passover.

- Adding a prayer for dew to the *Amidah Musaf* prayer on the first day of Passover to replace the prayer for rain, which was added on Shemini Atzeret. *Tal*, a prayer written by the poet Eleazar Kalir, is a reminder of the agricultural connections to the land of Israel, where the rainy season has ended but moisture is still needed.

Hiddur Mitzvah (Enhancing the Holiday)

One of the best ways to add to the enjoyment and appreciation of Passover is to begin a collection of Haggadot. There are many kinds of Haggadot available, including those of Jews from different lands, feminist Haggadot, and historical Haggadot such as the Sarajevo Haggadah. Many have excellent commentaries and are superbly illustrated. Beautiful Haggadot, such as the Szyk Haggadah, the

The Hebrew words Pesah, Matzah, *and* Maror *on the plate refer to the three principal symbols of the seder table—the paschal lamb, the unleavened bread, and the bitter herbs.*

Feast of History by Chaim Raphael, or the Ashkenazi Haggadah, with its Hebrew illuminated manuscripts, make wonderful gifts.

An exquisite cup of Elijah can also be a wonderful addition to a seder table. It could be made of crystal, china, silver, or glass.

Acquiring something special each year for the seder is a wonderful way to enhance the holiday. A lovely matzah cover or unusual seder plate can add immensely to the beauty of the seder table.

THIRTEEN WAYS TO ENRICH A SEDER

1. Invite a new immigrant, a single person, a new neighbor, someone new to the community, or someone without family nearby to your seder.
2. Have children prepare a skit to reenact a story or section from the Haggadah. My own children reenacted the section of "In every generation": one became a master with a whip and the other a slave on hands and knees. At the end of their musical rendition, they jumped over a sign that said "border of Egypt." Involve the children whenever possible, and pace the seder with them in mind.
3. Ask each person invited to the seder to prepare an explanation, commentary, or to ask a question on the Haggadah or anything pertaining to the holiday. Involve the guests in order to make the seder more interesting, but only if they are comfortable with this.
4. Distribute Haggadot with commentaries and different readings, and ask for volunteers to read one aloud at the appropriate section.
5. Discuss a contemporary subject of humanitarian and Jewish concern (refugees, prejudice, or hunger, for example) and try to relate it in some way to Passover.
6. Discuss modern examples (political, social, economic, or religious) of enslavement and freedom.
7. Learn a new seder melody or tradition from a guest. From one brother-in-law, I learned to sing the last verse of the song *Ehad Mi Yode'a* ("Who Knows One?") in one breath, and from another brother-in-law to act out that song with hand motions, and to add sounds to *Had Gadya* ("One Kid").
8. Adopt a custom from a Jew from another country (such as Ethiopia, Persia, or Iraq) or another time. There is, for example, a Moroccan custom to reenact the Exodus by putting matzah over a shoulder and, with a staff in hand, getting up from the table and marching around; or an old Hasidic custom to jump over a pail of water to reenact the crossing of the Red Sea.
9. Create an original custom.
10. Use a new kind of vegetable for *karpas*, such as fiddlehead ferns or artichokes.
11. Try a bitter herb from a bitter lettuce such as endive or escarole.
12. Try a new recipe for *haroset*. Many Jewish cookbooks have a variety of *haroset* recipes from Jews in different countries.
13. Try a different kind of kosher wine—a Cabernet Sauvignon or a sweet Tokay, for example.

A woman carries *matzah shmurah—matzah that has been watched from reaping to baking so that it does not come into contact with moisture and therefore fermentation.*

Matzah, or unleavened bread, replaces regular bread on Passover.

SEDER MENU

The seder meal is the most sumptuous of all the Jewish holidays. Cooking for Passover is more challenging than normal cooking, when so many of the old staples change, but the results can be just as mouth-watering. All ingredients should conform to Passover regulations. The following menu is both traditional and creative, filling but not too heavy. This menu gives several choices for vegetarians.

Haroset
Chicken Soup with Matzo Balls
Vegetable Broth for Vegetarians
Mushrooms in Puff Shells
Boston Lettuce with Orange Dressing
Stuffed Breast of Veal or Roast Brisket or Individual Vegetable Kugels
New Potatoes with Dill
Vegetable Farfel
Tarragon Asparagus
Chocolate Roll or Raspberry Glacé Pie
Pecan Meringue Cookies
Fruit Platter: Pineapple, Strawberries, Melon, Peaches

Ashkenazic Haroset

When I was a child, I was the one who always made the haroset. Today, I still make it much the same way as I did when I was young. I chop the apples and nuts by hand, although a food processor can make the task of chopping nuts a lot easier.

- 2 large tart apples
- ½ cup walnuts
- ½ to 1 teaspoon cinnamon
- ¼ teaspoon powdered ginger
- 1 tablespoon honey
- 2 tablespoons sweet red Passover wine

Peel and core apples. Chop apples and nuts together. Stir in cinnamon, ginger, honey, and wine.

Serves 10 to 12.

Sephardic-style Haroset

- ½ cup dates
- ½ cup raisins
- ½ cup pecans
- 1 medium orange, peeled, seeded, and sectioned
- 1 teaspoon cinnamon
- 3 tablespoons sweet red Passover wine

Put all ingredients except wine in a food processor and process until coarsely chopped. Add wine and process until a fine paste is formed.

Serves 10 to 12.

Note: Moroccan-style variation: Increase dates to 1 cup, omit orange, and reduce wine to 1 to 2 tablespoons. Form into balls and refrigerate.

Chicken Soup with Matzo Balls

- 1 large pullet and giblets, cut up, plus extra thigh and leg
- Water to cover (approximately 4 quarts)
- 1 packet kosher for Passover chicken soup mix (optional)
- 1 large onion, scored
- 1 leek, top and green
- 2 parsnips, peeled
- 1 small white turnip
- 3 stalks celery, with leaves
- 4 large carrots, scraped and cut into pieces
- 1 sweet potato, cut in chunks
- 10 sprigs fresh parsley
- 5 sprigs fresh dill
- Salt to taste
- Pepper to taste

Place chicken and giblets in large pot. Cover with water and bring to a boil. Skim off foam. Add soup mix and stir to dissolve. Add vegetables, fresh herbs, salt, and pepper. Cover and simmer approximately 2 to 3 hours or until chicken is tender. Correct seasoning. Strain soup, reserving carrots. Reheat, with carrots, until very hot. Serve with matzo balls and soup mandlen.

Serves 10 to 12.

Note: Adding a little instant Kosher chicken soup mix or broth gives this soup added body.

Matzo Balls (Kneidlach)

- ¼ cup oil
- 4 eggs, lightly beaten
- 1 cup matzo meal
- 1 teaspoon salt
- ¼ to ½ teaspoon ground ginger
- ¼ teaspoon onion powder (optional)
- ¼ cup water
- 2 to 3 tablespoons finely chopped parsley

Mix oil and eggs together. Add matzo meal, salt, ginger, and onion powder (if using). Mix well. Blend in water and parsley. Cover and refrigerate for 20 to 30 minutes. During this time bring a pot of water to boil. Form the mixture into small balls and drop into boiling water. Cover and cook over low heat 30 to 35 minutes. With slotted spoon, remove from pot and drop into soup, which is at room temperature.

Serves 10 to 12.

Vegetable Broth for Vegetarians

This vegetable broth is a good choice for vegetarians at the seder and can be used as a base for many other soup recipes requiring vegetable stock.

- 2 quarts water
- 1 large onion, cut into pieces
- 2 large carrots, peeled and sliced
- 4 ribs celery, with leaves, cut into large pieces
- 2 tomatoes, halved
- ¾ pound cabbage, cut into pieces
- 1 3-inch piece ginger, coarsely chopped
- 6 to 8 mushrooms, halved
- 6 cloves garlic, with skins
- 8 sprigs parsley
- Whole black peppercorns
- Whole cloves
- ½ teaspoon salt
- 1 large bay leaf

Put all ingredients in a large pot and bring to a boil. Lower heat and simmer for about 2 hours. Strain through cheesecloth and serve with matzo balls.

Serves 10 to 12.

Chicken Soup with Matzo Balls.

Mushrooms in Puff Shells

- 1½ cups boiling water
- ½ cup peanut oil
- ¾ teaspoon salt
- 1 tablespoon sugar
- 1½ cups cake meal
- 6 eggs

Preheat oven to 400 degrees F and spray two cookie sheets with nonstick Passover spray, or oil well.

In a large saucepan, combine boiling water, oil, salt, and sugar, and slowly bring to a boil. Reduce heat. Quickly add the cake meal and stir over low heat until mixture forms a ball. Remove from heat and add eggs one at a time, beating thoroughly after each addition. Drop by heaping tablespoonfuls onto greased cookie sheets and bake about 40 minutes. Cool. Cut off tops and remove excess dough from the middle. Place both tops and bottoms in oven for a minute or two to dry out. Fill with mushroom filling and replace tops.

Mushroom filling

- 2 pounds mixed mushrooms (regular, chanterelle, shiitake, crimini, porcini)
- 4 tablespoons sweet Passover margarine
- ¼ cup dry white Passover wine or Passover sherry
- 2 tablespoons potato starch
- 1 cup chicken stock, canned Passover chicken soup, or 1 teaspoon pareve chicken soup mix dissolved in 1 cup water
- Salt to taste
- Pepper to taste
- Garlic powder to taste

Clean mushrooms with a mushroom brush or towel. Cut base of stems of mushrooms. Cut large mushrooms into bite-size pieces and cut smaller ones in half. Heat margarine in saucepan. Add mushrooms and sauté for 3 minutes, or until they start to become soft. Add wine. Mix potato starch with a few tablespoons of stock or water. Add this with rest of the stock or water to mushroom mixture.

Boston Lettuce with Orange Dressing.

Season to taste. Cook several minutes until mixture thickens. Spoon into puff shells and serve.

Serves 10 to 12.

Boston Lettuce with Orange Dressing

- 3 heads Boston lettuce
- 3 heads Bibb lettuce
- 4 navel oranges, peeled and with white pith removed, quartered lengthwise, and sliced crosswise
- 1 red onion, thinly sliced
- ⅓ cup slivered almonds

Arrange lettuce with larger leaves on the bottom and smaller ones on top in rosette form. Top with oranges, onion, and almonds. Serve with orange dressing.
Serves 10 to 12.

Orange Dressing

- ⅓ cup orange juice
- ⅓ cup peanut oil
- ¼ teaspoon salt
- Pepper to taste
- Dash of cinnamon

Combine all ingredients and pour over salad.

Stuffed Breast of Veal

- 1 7-pound breast of veal with pocket
- Minced garlic
- Fresh thyme
- Salt to taste
- Paprika to taste
- Pepper to taste
- 2 onions, sliced
- 2 stalks celery, chopped
- 6 carrots, sliced
- 6 garlic cloves, unpeeled
- ½ cup Passover white wine
- ½ cup water

Filling

- 1 medium onion, diced
- 1½ pounds minced veal
- 1 tablespoon Passover margarine
- 2 tablespoons Passover ketchup
- ½ teaspoon garlic powder
- ¾ teaspoon salt
- ⅛ teaspoon pepper
- ¼ cup parsley
- ½ cup matzo meal
- ½ to 1 cup Passover white wine

Preheat oven to 350 degrees F. Wash veal with cold water and pat dry. Season veal with minced garlic, thyme, salt, paprika, and pepper.

Mix filling ingredients by sautéing onion in margarine. Add to minced veal along with ketchup, garlic powder, salt, pepper, parsley, matzo meal, and wine to moisten. Stuff veal and sew pocket. Put in a roasting pan. Add an equal amount of wine and water to the bottom of the roasting pan and scatter with onion, celery, and carrots. Cover and roast for about 3 hours. Remove cover the last half hour to brown. When cool, slice, remove large bones, and put it back together. Place in a serving dish. Strain juices and skim fat for gravy.

Serves 10 to 12.

Note: Veal may also be braised first in hot oil and then placed in roasting pan.

Roast Brisket

When living in Nashville, Tennessee, I learned how to produce a tender brisket from the cantor's wife, Anna Glusman. She roasted it in a cooking bag.

- 4- to 5-pound brisket, first cut
- 1 teaspoon garlic powder
- 1 teaspoon salt
- ½ teaspoon ginger
- 1 teaspoon freshly ground pepper
- 1 clove garlic, halved
- 1 cup Passover sherry
- 1 cup Passover ketchup
- 2 to 3 tablespoons Passover brown sugar
- 1 tablespoon potato starch
- 1 large onion, sliced

Preheat oven to 325 degrees F.

Combine garlic powder, salt, ginger, pepper, and garlic and rub into meat. Combine sherry, ketchup, and brown sugar. Place meat in an oven bag with 1 tablespoon potato starch. Pour sauce over meat and add onion. Put bag in roasting pan. Make 6 slits in bag, according to the directions on the package. Roast for 2½ to 3 hours, or until tender. Strain juices from bag and serve as gravy. Garnish with steamed carrots.

Serves 10 to 12.

Note: If a roasting bag is not available, season meat, then sear it in 1 tablespoon of vegetable oil. Drain off excess oil. Add sauce. Cover, and place in oven and roast at 325 degrees F for 2½ to 3 hours.

Individual Vegetable Kugels

My friend Susan Mandelbaum shared this recipe with me. It is excellent for vegetarians on Passover and all year round.

- 3 tablespoons Passover margarine
- 1 medium onion, chopped
- 1 large stalk celery, chopped (½ cup)
- 3 large carrots, grated (1½ cups)
- ¼ cup chopped red pepper
- ¼ cup chopped green pepper
- 1 10-ounce package frozen spinach, cooked and well drained
- 3 eggs, well beaten
- 1 teaspoon salt
- ¼ teaspoon freshly ground nutmeg (optional)
- **Fresh pepper to taste**
- ⅔ cup matzo meal

Preheat oven to 375 degrees F and grease or spray 12 muffin tins or disposable custard containers with nonstick coating. Heat margarine in a saucepan and sauté onion, celery, carrots, and peppers for a few minutes, until onion is translucent. Set aside.

Put well-drained spinach in a bowl. Add eggs, salt, nutmeg, and pepper. Mix thoroughly. Add sautéed vegetables and matzo meal. Mix well. Spoon into custard pans or muffin tins. Bake for 35 to 40 minutes. Cool 10 to 15 minutes before removing from custard pan or muffin tin.

Makes 12 kugels.

New Potatoes with Dill.

New Potatoes with Dill

- 3 pounds new potatoes
- 2 teaspoons chopped fresh dill
- ¼ to ⅓ cup oil
- 3 tablespoons fresh lemon juice
- Salt to taste
- Pepper to taste

Thinly slice new potatoes, leaving skins on. Toss in mixture of dill, oil, lemon juice, salt, and pepper. Put into well-oiled casserole pan and roast in 450 degree F oven for approximately 25 minutes, turning occasionally until brown. Serve immediately or reheat in 350 degree F oven.

Serves 10 to 12.

Note: The new potatoes can also be diced or roasted whole, coated with the lemon, oil, and dill mixture.

Sliced Roast Brisket.

Tarragon Asparagus.

Vegetable Farfel

Farfel can be served as a rice substitute on Passover.

- ¼ cup Passover margarine
- 3 large onions, minced
- 5¼ cups matzo farfel
- ½ green pepper, finely chopped
- ½ red pepper, finely chopped
- 1½ teaspoons salt
- ¼ teaspoon pepper
- 1 teaspoon paprika
- ¾ teaspoon poultry seasoning
- 3 seasoning packets or 3 teaspoons of pareve chicken soup mix
- 3¾ cups boiling water

Melt margarine in a large skillet and sauté onions until tender. Add the matzo farfel and stir until lightly browned. Combine seasonings with boiling water. Add slowly to skillet and cook until water is absorbed.

Serves 10 to 12.

Tarragon Asparagus

Fresh bright green asparagus is a perfect seder vegetable.

- 3 pounds asparagus spears
- Water
- Salt to taste
- 2 tablespoons Passover margarine
- 3 tablespoons chopped scallions
- 1 tablespoon snipped fresh tarragon
- 2 tablespoons fresh parsley
- 1 tablespoon lemon juice

Snap off the fibrous asparagus ends. Fill a pan large enough to accommodate the asparagus with water. Add salt and bring to a boil. Add asparagus and cover. When water boils again, uncover and cook until crisp-tender, about 4 minutes, depending on thickness of asparagus. Do not overcook. Drain immediately. Melt margarine in skillet. Add scallions, tarragon, parsley, and lemon juice. Spoon over asparagus and serve.

Serves 10 to 12.

Note: Asparagus may also be steamed by filling pot with 1 inch of water brought to a boil and placing asparagus in a steamer rack set over the water.

Chocolate Roll

The recipe for this rich, irresistible chocolate roll was given to me by Judy Wahler of Caldwell, New Jersey. It goes well with a whipped cream filling, but for Passover purposes I have included a chocolate filling, since pareve whipped topping is often unavailable for Passover.

- 8 ounces sweet or semisweet Passover chocolate
- ½ teaspoon powdered coffee
- 3 tablespoons warm water
- 5 large eggs, separated
- 1 cup sugar
- 1 teaspoon Passover vanilla
- Passover cocoa

Heat oven to 375 degrees F. Oil a jelly roll pan with cooking oil or nonstick Passover spray. Cut waxed paper to line pan with a 1-inch overlap on each side. Oil or spray the paper, including the sides. Melt chocolate in a double boiler. Remove from heat. Dissolve coffee in warm water and add to chocolate. Add sugar to the egg yolks and beat until sugar is dissolved. Add vanilla. Blend in cooled chocolate mixture. Beat egg whites until stiff but not dry, and fold into chocolate until white streaks disappear. Turn egg whites into oiled jelly roll pan and bake at 375 degrees F for 5 minutes. Reduce oven to 350 degrees F and bake 10 more minutes or until toothpick in center comes out dry. Wet a dish towel, wring it dry, and cover the chocolate roll for 10 to 20 minutes. Flip cake onto two sides of overlapping sheets of waxed paper dusted with cocoa (confectioners' sugar when it's not Passover). Fill with chocolate filling (recipe below) and roll either lengthwise or widthwise. Cake may crack. Refrigerate or freeze until ready to serve.

Serves 10 if rolled lengthwise.

Chocolate Filling

- 3 1-ounce squares bittersweet Passover chocolate
- ½ cup Passover margarine
- ½ cup extra-fine granulated sugar
- 1 teaspoon Passover vanilla
- 2 eggs

Melt chocolate in double boiler or over very low heat. Set aside to cool. Beat margarine until creamy. Add sugar and continue beating until light and fluffy. Add cooled chocolate and vanilla and mix well. Add eggs one at a time, beating well after each addition until mixture is smooth. Let harden slightly in refrigerator. Spread over cake.

Whipped Cream Filling (for dairy meal)

- ½ pint whipped cream or nondairy kosher-for-Passover topping (if available)
- 2 tablespoons superfine sugar (confectioners' sugar, which contains cornstarch, if it's not Passover)
- 1 teaspoon Passover vanilla or other flavoring

Whip cream until soft peaks form. Add sugar slowly, then vanilla or other flavoring. Spread on chocolate roll.

Raspberry Glacé Pie

Fresh raspberries are delicious in this recipe, as are fresh blueberries and strawberries. This is a light dessert after a heavy seder meal.

Meringue shell
- 2 egg whites at room temperature
- ½ cup superfine sugar
- Pinch of salt
- 1 teaspoon lemon juice

Beat egg whites and salt until foamy. Slowly add sugar one tablespoon at a time while beating on high speed. Add lemon juice. Beat until very stiff and glossy. Spread meringue into a lightly greased 9-inch pie shell and bake in 250 degree F oven for 1 hour. When cool, fill with raspberry glacé filling (recipe below).

Raspberry glacé filling
- 2 tablespoons potato starch
- 2 tablespoons water
- 1 teaspoon lemon juice
- 1 quart (4 cups) fresh raspberries (or blueberries or strawberries)
- ½ cup water
- 1 tablespoon Passover margarine
- ¾ cup sugar

Mix together potato starch, water, and lemon juice and stir until potato starch is dissolved. Place 1 cup raspberries and ½ cup water in a medium saucepan and bring to a boil. Add potato starch mixture, margarine, and sugar. Stir until mixture is thick and clear. Place remaining berries into baked meringue shell and pour glaze over. Refrigerate until set.

Serves 8.

Pecan Meringue Cookies

These are good for Passover and all year round. Meringue cookies are easy when made with superfine or instant sugar added gradually to egg whites and baked on parchment paper.

- 2 egg whites
- Dash of salt
- 1 teaspoon Passover vanilla
- ⅔ cup superfine or regular granulated sugar
- 1 cup chopped pecans
- ¾ cup Passover chocolate chips (optional)

Preheat oven to 250 degrees F. Cover cookie sheets with parchment paper.

At high speed, beat egg whites and salt until frothy. Gradually add sugar, approximately 2 tablespoons at a time, beating well after each addition, until mixture is stiff and shiny and stands in peaks. Fold in vanilla, pecans and, if desired, chocolate chips.

Drop meringues by teaspoonfuls onto cookie sheets. Bake for 30 minutes.

Makes about 2 dozen cookies.

Variation: For seder mint meringue cookies, omit pecans and chocolate chips and fold in 1 cup coarsely chopped seder mints or Passover peppermint patties.

Raspberry Glacé Pie.

SHAVUOT

After their physical liberation from bondage to freedom, and the birth of nationhood commemorated by the festival of Passover, Jews begin to look forward to their spiritual redemption on Shavuot, to their acceptance of the responsibility that freedom brings.

The seven-week countdown from Passover to Shavuot (which means "weeks") is known as *Sefirat Haomer*. The omer is the bridge between the two major festivals. The festival of Shavuot falls on the fiftieth day, called Pentecost in English. In the Talmud, Shavuot is known as *Atzeret*, for the sages saw it as the conclusion of Passover, much as *Shemini Atzeret* was seen as the conclusion of Sukkot. Yet both "*Atzerets*" are actually independent holidays.

Since no specific date is designated for the celebration of Shavuot in the Bible, a debate ensued between the Pharisees and Sadducees (Jewish political and religious parties during the second Temple period) as to when Shavuot should take place. The Bible says, "And you shall count from the day after the Sabbath from the day on which you bring the sheaf of waving seven complete weeks" (Lev. 23:15–16). It is unclear from the text what was meant by the "day after the Sabbath." Did the Sabbath refer literally to the Sabbath of Passover, as the Sadducees thought—which would make

Shavuot always fall on a Sunday—or did it refer to a day when no work was done? The Pharisees decided that the Sabbath referred to the former, to the first day of Passover, and it became accepted tradition to count the omer from the second day of Passover, setting a fixed date for the holiday on the sixth of Sivan. It is interesting to note that Ethiopian Jews, who knew nothing of rabbinic tradition, celebrated Shavuot on the twelfth of Sivan, for they understood the Sabbath to mean the last day of Passover. Today, traditional Jews in the Diaspora celebrate Shavuot for two days—on the sixth and seventh of Sivan—while Reform Jews and those living in Israel observe the holiday on the sixth of Sivan only.

Opposite: Women collecting sheaves of wheat in the hills of Judea as Ruth did in the fields of Boaz. Left: This imaginative Shavuot woodcut from Sefer Minhagim, the Book of Customs (Amsterdam 1723), depicts Moses on Mount Sinai receiving the Tablets of the Law.

THE OMER

The word *omer* literally means a specific measure of barley from the barley harvest that was to be brought to the priest in the Temple in Jerusalem on the sixteenth day of the month of Nisan. This measure of barley was elaborately prepared, and in a vivid and colorful ceremony given to the priest for the ritual of "waving." As the Priest waved the omer back and forth and sideways, those assembled understood that ritual to be a prayer before God to protect the coming harvest from bad weather.

For as long as the Temple was in existence, the omer was presented to the Priest. In addition, the days between Passover and the festival of Shavuot were counted, day by day, for forty-nine days. Consequently, this entire period between Passover and Shavuot is called *Sefirat Haomer*, the "counting of the omer," or the *sefirah*, for short.

Once the Temple was destroyed, however, the omer could no longer be presented to the Priest. The idea of the omer and the counting of the days between Passover and Shavuot were in danger of being forgotten. The Rabbis, always inventive, wanted to perpetuate the ritual of the count, and recast "the counting." They made it part of the daily liturgy, together with a blessing. Thus, everyone began enumerating the omer beginning with the evening of the fifteenth day of Nisan until the completion of seven full weeks, forty-nine days, with the holiday of Shavuot commencing on the fiftieth day.

Later rabbinic authorities, eager to find new meaning in the idea of the *sefirah*, considered the forty-nine days as "seven times seven" (seven being a perfect number), while kabbalists saw in the multiples of seven the concept of the *sefirot* or the forty-nine gates of impurity from which Israel was released as it left Egypt.

According to a very old tradition, the period between Passover and Shavuot is a season of mourning. Marriages are not performed during this period, hair is not cut, and music is not played or heard. The reasons for this are not clear. Some suggest that a plague cost the lives of many of Rabbi Akiba's students during the Roman period and that on the thirty-third day of the omer, the plague suddenly ceased. Hence, the establishment of a special Lag Baomer (literally, "thirty-third day of the omer") celebration.

Another tradition suggests that since this period was preparatory to receiving the Torah, these days should be set aside for reflection, study, and rededication to the principles of Jewish life and ritual. Therefore, frivolous activities were to be avoided. Today, the twenty-seventh of Nisan, which falls on the twelfth day of the omer, has been set aside as *Yom Hashoah*, or Holocaust Remembrance Day.

Whatever the case may be, the counting of the days of the omer has now become a numerical link between the two major festivals of Passover and Shavuot and a timely contemporary reminder to count every day, because every day counts.

Left: A wall omer counter showing the days of the omer, which link the major festivals of Passover and Shavuot. Above: An artistic seventeenth-century omer scroll from Holland written with ink and paint on parchment enumerates the days of the omer.

SHAVUOT AS AN AGRICULTURAL HOLIDAY

In the Bible, Shavuot is strictly an agricultural festival known as *Hag Hakatzir* (Harvest Holiday)—the celebration of the end of the barley harvest and the beginning of the wheat harvest. Along with Passover and Sukkot, it is one of the three harvest festivals.

On Shavuot, two loaves of wheat bread from choice first wheat crops were baked and offered by priests at the Temple in Jerusalem as offerings of thanksgiving. Shavuot is also called *Yom Habikkurim* (Day of First Fruits), to commemorate the bringing of first fruits of the seven species (wheat, barley, grapes, figs, pomegranates, olives, and dates) to the Temple in Jerusalem. This vivid ceremony, described in elaborate detail in the Mishnah, marks the beginning of a new agricultural season.

SHAVUOT AS A SPIRITUAL HOLIDAY

If Shavuot had remained a purely agricultural holiday, with no historical event attached to it—as the Exodus from Egypt is attached to Passover and the ancient Israelites wandering in the desert living in temporary dwellings is attached to Sukkot—the holiday would have surely died out. Recognizing this, the Rabbis wisely attached one of the greatest of all historical events to Shavuot, thereby ensuring its survival. By the third century, Shavuot became known as "the time of the giving of the Torah" at Sinai, giving the holiday an essential spiritual component, and linking it to the Exodus and Israel's journey to the promised land.

Despite this, Shavuot is a major holiday that has had a minor impact. Shavuot has no central ritual and today few special rituals associated with it and, as a result, remains the least known and the least observed of the major Jewish festivals. Its central concept is the commemoration of revelation (God revealing Himself) at Mount Sinai and the celebration of the covenantal relationship between God and Israel, symbolized by the giving of the Torah. These are difficult and esoteric concepts for most people to grasp. Nonetheless, Shavuot is an extremely compelling holiday, because it celebrates a singular event in ancient Jewish history.

What happened at Mount Sinai was preceded by a covenantal relationship between God and Israel, a mutual commitment by the two parties pledging eternal faithfulness, much as a marriage—a popular metaphor in the Bible—in which Israel is depicted as the bride and God the bridegroom. "And I will betroth you unto me forever" (Hos. 2:1). The marriage that took place at Mount Sinai between the children of Israel and God was sealed with the words "we will do and we will hear." These words committed the Israelites

Kibbutz children decked with garlands on their heads and dressed in white sit on decorated wagons to celebrate Shavuot as a holiday of bikkurim—first fruit.

SALEINU*
Decked with Garlands

Sa - lei - nu al k'tei - fei - nu,   ro - shei - nu a - tu - rim
Our heads are decked with gar - lands, Bas - kets heaped to the brim

Mi - k'tsot ha - a - rets ba - nu,   hei - vei - nu bi - ku - rim.
From far and near we're com-ing, We're bring - ing "Bi - ku - rim."

Mi - Y'hu - da,   mi - Y'hu - da__ umi - Shom - ron,
From the E - mek, From the Jor - dan and Sha - ron,

Min ha - Ei - mek,   min ha - Ei - mek, v'ha - Ga - lil.
From Ju - de - a, From Ga - lil and the Her - mon;

Pa - nu de - rech la - nu;   bi - ku - rim i - ta - nu,
Clear ye, clear the way, __This is pil-grims day.__

Hah, hah, hah ba - tof,   v'ha - leil be - cha - lil! __v'ha - leil be - cha - lil!
Beat, beat, beat the drum, Sound the flute and sing, __First of fruits we bring.

Lyrics by L. Kipnis; music by J. Admon
© Tarbut Vechinuch ED., ACUM, Israel.

*See music on page 119.

WHAT IS TORAH?

In the synagogue, housed in an ark, are scrolls covered by cloth mantles and adorned with silver crowns and breastplates. Each scroll is a handwritten parchment copy in Hebrew of the Five Books of Moses (Genesis, Exodus, Leviticus, Numbers, and Deuteronomy). These scrolls are considered among the most sacred objects within Jewish tradition. Every Shabbat, on all holidays, and on Monday and Thursday mornings, a selection from one of the scrolls is read for the congregation. This is Torah in its narrowest definition.

Torah also refers to the rest of the Hebrew Bible, including the earlier and later prophets, and writings such as the Psalms and the *megillot*. All in all, thirty-nine books (twenty-four according to traditional count) make up what is known as "the written Torah" (*Torah shebikhtav*) or written law.

Another tradition was also given to the people of Israel: the "oral law" (*Torah sheb'al peh*). Together, the written and oral law are known as *Torah mishamayim*—Torah from heaven, meaning Divinely ordained and sanctioned. Oral law added to, expanded, and explained the written law so that Scripture always remained fresh and new. These explanations and interpretations began almost immediately after Moses received the law from Mount Sinai. Many Jews think that these interpretations were given to Moses at Sinai simultaneously with the written law and were handed down orally from generation to generation. Other Jews believe that the explanations and interpretations of the written law were developed by each generation as it studied the written Torah.

Whether God revealed the written and oral law simultaneously, or whether the oral law was the outgrowth of the careful study of the written law, the interpretations and explanations were eventually written down so that they would not be forgotten. This became the Mishnah, laws which became codes of behavior and descriptions of rituals. No sooner did the Mishnah become a written code (approximately 200 C.E.), then further discussions developed among the Rabbis as to the meaning and application of the Mishnah. These discussions were also recorded and became known as the Gemara. Together, the Mishnah and the Gemara are known as the Talmud, a vast and complicated body of work that is studied by learned Jews to this day. The Talmud is also included in the word "Torah."

Thus the Torah is more than just the scrolls found in the ark of a synagogue and more than the rest of the Hebrew Bible that followed,

Above left: A Torah shield from Prague. Above: A nineteenth-century Torah scroll from Iraq in its original silver housing. Below left: Torah pointers used during the reading of the Torah. Below right: A Torah crown from Prague used to adorn the Torah.

even more than the Talmud, the Responsa literature (rabbinic replies to inquiries on religious questions), and the explanations and interpretations that the Rabbis added to and that are argued over until the present day. Torah, which also means "instruction," is the living embodiment of a whole people engaged in the study of all these texts, trying to determine how to live a good and sacred life.

Jews therefore approach Torah with a special love, devotion, and feeling of sanctity. It is called a "tree of life to those who hold fast to it." Each letter is considered holy; no word is without purpose. There is nothing extraneous in the Torah. Ferreting out its meaning and relaying its message from one generation to the next has brought joy and challenge to Jews for thousands of years.

to an ethical and moral code that was not only binding on them, but on all future generations of Jews. Sephardic Jews have created an actual marriage document, or *ketubah*, for Shavuot, which specifies the obligations between Israel and God, thus giving concrete expression to an abstract idea.

There is a classic midrash explaining that God offered the Torah to the other nations of the world, all of whom rejected it for various reasons when they were told of its contents. It was only Israel who unconditionally accepted the Torah without even knowing its contents, and were its willing and eager recipients.

A contrasting midrash describes God as holding up the mountain of Sinai over the heads of the Israelites, forcing them to accept the Torah lest it become their grave. The tradition clearly emphasizes that the children of Israel did not receive the Torah for any inherent merit that they possessed. The Torah was given as a responsibility to the Jewish people to practice and lead a sanctified and ethical life and to serve as an example to others. For the Jewish people, the Torah has been the repository of wisdom and their constitution for thousands of years, a symbol of their commitment to a specific way of life and living.

Nowhere is this commitment more apparent than in the *megillah* reading designated for Shavuot, known as *Megillat Rut*, the Book of Ruth. A lovely, pastoral short story, the Book of Ruth describes how the young Moabite widow Ruth unconditionally embraces the faith and people of her mother-in-law, Naomi, saying "Do not urge me to leave you, to turn back and not follow you. For wherever you go, I will go; wherever you lodge, I will lodge; your people shall be my people and your God, my God" (Ruth 1:16). (Today, these words form part of the Jewish conversion ceremony.) The story takes place during the barley and wheat harvest season, which is another reason the Rabbis chose to read the Book of Ruth on Shavuot. In addition, Ruth was supposedly the ancestor of King David, who, according to tradition, was born and died on Shavuot. Because tradition ascribes the authorship of the Psalms to King David, it is customary to read psalms on Shavuot that depict a profound depth of religious fervor and devotion.

The Torah reading for the first day of Shavuot is the description of the giving of the Torah on Mount Sinai, including the Ten Commandments. It is customary in many synagogues for people to stand when that portion is read, as if they were once again standing at Sinai accepting those commandments. Although the practice was rejected by some rabbinic authorities who did not like the idea of singling out one section of Torah over another, the practice remains in most synagogues today.

The Haftarah, or prophetic reading, for the first day of Shavuot is from the first chapter of the Book of Ezekiel plus an additional verse from the third chapter. It portrays a rather bizarre vision, perhaps suggesting that mystical visions are unique and highly personal. Each person understands and embraces God and Torah differently.

SHAVUOT PRACTICES

An especially lovely tradition associated with Shavuot and borrowed from the kabbalists is *Tikkun Leil Shavuot*—the service for the evening of Shavuot. As a way of intensely experiencing the Torah in preparation for the first day of the holiday, learned and pious Jews study Torah all night. The kabbalists devised a special order of study that comprised selections from each book of the Bible, the Talmud, and mystical literature. One of the reasons for this tradition is that the children of Israel were said to be asleep when God appeared on Mount Sinai. To ensure that this would

THE MYRIAD ANGELS' SONGS

Jacob Ben Meir

The following poem is chanted by Sephardic Jews on Shavuot, after the first verse of the haftarah is read. The poem is in acrostic style and contains the author's name.

The myriad angels' songs of praise
On high have loudly pealed;
  On earth I too am glorying
  God's Law this day revealed.
A stream of flame goes forth from Him
Toward the watery flood.
  A light shines on a mount of snow
  With flames as red as blood.
Creator He, He sees through dark.
He is the source of light;
  He sees afar with nought to bar;
  To Him the dark shines bright.
Approval for my song I ask
Of Him, and of those versed
  In books derived from Scripture's text
  And codes from last to first.
Guard Thou, O ever-living King,
Thy people seeking Thee;
  Make them to be as dust of earth,
  And as the sand of sea.
Yea, may their valleys shine with flocks,
Their presses flow with wine,
  And grant their prayer, and make their face
  As radiant sun to shine.
Let me be strong. Weak must they be
Whose life by Thee is blamed.
  May they be dumb as inmost stone,
  May they be ever shamed,
For Moses, meekest of all men,
Gave us Thy Torah famed.

Translated by David de Sola Pool, from *The Traditional Prayer Book for Sabbath and Festivals*, published by Berman House, Inc. Used with permission.

THE SCROLLS OF RUTH AND ESTHER

Of the five *megillot*, or scrolls, found in the Bible, three have no sharply defined characters. Only two are named after persons and both are women: Ruth and Esther. These two remarkable women would be unusual in any age. Their stories are read on the holidays of Shavuot and Purim, respectively.

The stories start identically. The Book of Ruth begins with the words "And it happened in the days of the Judges," and the Scroll of Esther begins with "And it happened in the days of Ahasuerus." Both scrolls originate in what would appear to be the male dominance of history, one pastoral and rustic, the other urbane and sophisticated.

Both Ruth and Esther confront a brand-new world as virtual strangers in a strange land: Ruth, a Moabite native among the Israelites; Esther, a Jew in the Persian court. Both are aliens: Ruth must learn the customs of Israel; Esther is a "closet" Jew who must learn to maneuver through the often complicated ways of a pagan court.

In simple but clever ways, Ruth enchants the provincial world of Bethlehem. Not only does she gather sheaves to keep body and soul together, but she also manages to find her way into the field of Boaz, Naomi's pious and noble kinsman, and eventually into his heart. Esther, on the other hand, enchants an urbane and wealthy court with her beauty and courage, and becomes a queen to Ahasuerus, king of Persia.

Both Ruth and Esther unabashedly use their womanly charms to achieve security not for themselves, but for their people. Ruth comes to Boaz, late in the night during the threshing season, sleeps by his feet until he awakens, and then establishes a relationship that culminates in marriage. She becomes the ancestor of King David, the royal house that became a metaphor for all royalty and nobility in Israel. Esther, through her womanly charms, is able to unmask the evil Haman with his dread desire to kill all the Jews of Persia. She thereby saves her people from certain destruction and ensures the survival of the Jewish people in Persia.

Most important, both Ruth and Esther act independently, assertively, and with great wisdom. Against the wishes of her mother-in-law, Naomi, Ruth remains with her, traveling to a new country and creating a new life. Something in her mother-in-law and her religion appealed to Ruth's innermost heart. She gave up the wealth of Moab with its physical comforts, and instead chose the spiritual riches of Israel and lived in poverty.

Esther, too, acted with fortitude and courage. When told by Mordecai of Haman's plan to murder all the Jews of Persia, she decreed a national fast for her people. The king had left strict instructions that he not be disturbed on pain of death; Esther risked her easy and secure life at court (she had not revealed her religion to anyone) and boldly came to the king, knowing full well that if she failed, she and her people would be destroyed.

These were exceptional women, unusual for their beauty, grace, and courage. Little wonder that their names are titles to their stories. In contrast, the men of these scrolls play secondary roles. Some of them were noble, such as Mordecai and Boaz, and some were ignoble, such as Elimelech and Haman. Ruth and Esther, on the other hand, are the clear masters and architects of their lives. They stake their own claim on life, play key roles in the lives of their community, and consequently transform the future of their people.

Ruth gleaning sheaves of wheat in the fields of Boaz.

never happen again and to make amends, extra vigilance is exercised by studying all night. There is also a mystical explanation that it is like preparing the bride before the wedding.

Studying and Shavuot go hand in hand because of the holiday's association with Torah. In France and Germany, Shavuot was the time that young children were brought into the classroom for the first time and given slates on which were written Hebrew letters covered with honey to lick off and sweets to eat, making their introduction to Torah study a sweet and delectable one. A more recent custom instituted by the Reform branch of Judaism is the confirmation ceremony, which was originally intended to replace the bar mitzvah ceremony. Instead, it has become an adjunct to that ceremony for high school youngsters and marks the end of their formal religious education. Today, many Reform and Conservative synagogues hold confirmation ceremonies on Shavuot.

It is not altogether clear why dairy dishes are served on Shavuot, but several theories have been suggested. Some cite the verse in the Song of Songs "Honey and milk are on your tongue" (Song of Songs 4:11), which is said to refer to Torah. Others say that after the children of Israel returned from Sinai, they were too tired and hungry to wait for a meat meal and therefore ate dairy products. Still another explanation is that when the Israelites returned from Sinai, they had just received the laws of kashrut and had to make their utensils kosher, so they ate dairy food in the meantime.

The whiteness of milk can be seen as a symbol of the purity of the Torah. It may also be that eating dairy is of a higher order than eating meat. The laws of kashrut teach that meat was given as a concession, not as an ideal. Adam, who inhabited the Garden of Eden, was a vegetarian. Human beings were not meant to be carnivorous and Scripture suggests will not be in the future. On the holiday to honor the Torah, one aspires to the ideal.

SHAVUOT AND NATURE

Shavuot as an agricultural holiday is much in evidence in many synagogues and homes, which are bedecked with foliage and fresh flowers. This custom is based on a midrash describing Mount Sinai at the time the Torah was given as resplendent with grass and trees. Moreover, according to the Talmud, Shavuot was thought to be the judgment day for the trees.

On Shavuot, nature and the Divine go hand in hand. After all, nature for Jews is but an expression of the Divine and needs tending and reseeding so that there can be re-creation. As nature is continually renewed, so Jews continue to renew themselves each year on Shavuot by listening afresh to the voice of Mount Sinai and rededicating themselves to the spiritual and ethical commitments that the Torah represents.

This painting by American folk artist Harry Lieberman is entitled The Harvest.

According to a Hasidic rabbi, the reason Shavuot is called the time of the giving of the Torah and not the time of receiving it is that while the Torah was given once at the time of Moses, it is continually being received. Although the moment of revelation that Mount Sinai commemorates lasted but a short while, the covenant and its renewal, Torah and its study are endlessly challenging and continuing processes that make Judaism forever fresh and vigorous.

PSALM 19

For the leader. A psalm of David.

The heavens declare the glory of God,
    the sky proclaims His handiwork.
Day to day makes utterance,
    night to night speaks out.
There is no utterance,
    there are no words,
    whose sound goes unheard.
Their voice carries throughout the earth,
    their words to the end of the world.
He placed in them a tent for the sun,
    who is like a groom coming forth from the chamber,
    like a hero, eager to run his course.
His rising-place is at one end of heaven,
    and his circuit reaches the other;
    nothing escapes his heat.

The teaching of the LORD is perfect,
    renewing life;
    the decrees of the LORD are enduring,
    making the simple wise;
The precepts of the LORD are just,
    rejoicing the heart;
    the instruction of the LORD is lucid,
    making the eyes light up.
The fear of the LORD is pure,
    abiding forever;
    the judgments of the LORD are true,
    righteous altogether,
    more desirable than gold,
    than much fine gold;
    sweeter than honey,
    than drippings of the comb.
Your servant pays them heed;
    in obeying them there is much reward.
Who can be aware of errors?
Clear me of unperceived guilt,
    and from willful sins keep Your servant;
    let them not dominate me;
    then shall I be blameless
    and clear of grave offense.
May the words of my mouth
    and the prayer of my heart
    be acceptable to You,
    O LORD, my rock and my redeemer.

TRADITIONS AND CUSTOMS ASSOCIATED WITH SHAVUOT

- Reading the Book of Ruth on the second day of Shavuot without blessings.
- Reading a special Aramaic ode called *Akdamut* or *Akdamut Millin* (meaning "introduction") written by Meir ben Isaac Nehorai, an eleventh-century cantor in Worms, Germany, before the Torah reading. The ninety-line acrostic poem with the author's name profusely praises God, acclaims the excellence of Torah, celebrates Israel's devotion to God and Torah, and describes Israel's glorious future.
- Reading liturgical poems called *azharot* on Shavuot. The *azharot* (meaning "warnings") recited most by Sephardic Jews are by the eleventh-century Spanish-Jewish poet Solomon Ibn Gabirol and incorporate the 613 commandments of the Torah.
- Spending the first night of Shavuot in study is a kabbalistic custom called *Tikkun Leil Shavuot*. Many Jews stay up all night studying Torah or other Jewish texts.
- Studying the Psalms (*Tehillim*) on the second night of Shavuot is a less common custom, but is done because King David, who is associated with Shavuot, is said to be its author.
- Eating dairy foods such as cheese blintzes and cheesecake.
- Decorating homes and synagogues with greenery and flowers commemorates Shavuot as an agricultural holiday.
- Baking extra-long hallah loaves on Shavuot to commemorate the two wheat bread offerings at the Temple.
- Kibbutzim in Israel hold ceremonies commemorating the "first fruits" with dancing, singing, and performances. Special processions include wagons and tractors of newly harvested produce, grain, eggs, and honey. Sometimes children dressed in white carry flowers and leaves.

Hiddur Mitzvah (Enhancing the Holiday)

Buy new indoor plants for your home on Shavuot, and plant some of the flowering plants in your garden after the holiday. Bring in from the garden whatever is seasonal and in bloom. Freshly cut flowers are always appropriate for Shavuot, especially roses; Shavuot was once called The Feast of Roses in Italy and Spain. At one time, garlands of roses bedecked the Torah, and paper cuts of flowers for Shavuot known as *raizlakh* (little roses) or *shavuoslakh* (little Shavuots) were a popular folk art form adorning home and synagogue.

Shavuot is a wonderful holiday for the vegetarian. It is an excellent time to try different kinds of dairy and vegetarian dishes. Experiment with all kinds of blintzes, crepes, kugels, roulades, pasta, and cheesecakes.

Dairy dishes, especially blintzes, are featured on the Shavuot table.

SHAVUOT MENU

The Shavuot menu is traditionally dairy—especially on the first day, when any type of vegetarian or dairy dish is appropriate. I have devised two menus so as to be able to include both cheese blintzes and cheesecake. The first menu has traditional cheese blintzes and its Italian and French counterparts—manicotti and crepes. The second, more sophisticated menu, has a fish dish and a white chocolate cheesecake. A platter of fresh and dried fruit recalls Shavuot's origins as a harvest festival.

Menu #1
Cold Cherry Soup
Baby Spinach Salad with Lemon Vinaigrette Dressing
Broccoli Mushroom Crepes
or Cheese Blintzes
or Spinach and Ricotta Manicotti with Tomato Sauce
Blueberry Streusel Coffee Cake
Rugelach

Menu #2
Ginger Carrot Soup
Broiled Halibut with Capers
Herbed Orzo
Sauteed Zucchini
White/Dark Chocolate Cheesecake
Fruit Platter: Strawberries, Watermelon, Nectarines, Dried Apricots, Dates, and Figs

Cold Cherry Soup.

Cold Cherry Soup

*Some make cherry soup with sweet cherries.
I like the tart blend of sour cherries and
sweet wine.*

- 2 1-pound cans of red cherries
  in water
- 1 cinnamon stick
- ¼ teaspoon allspice
- ¼ teaspoon ground cloves
- ¾ cup red wine
- 1 tablespoon cornstarch
- 2 tablespoons water
- ⅓ to ½ cup sugar

Drain cherries, reserving juice and 1 cup
of cherries. Place remainder of cherries in
saucepan. Add reserved cherry juice and
enough water to make 3 cups of liquid.
Add cinnamon stick and spices. Bring to a
boil. Reduce heat, cover, and simmer 10
minutes. Cool slightly. Process in blender
or food processor until smooth. Return to
saucepan. Add wine. Blend cornstarch
with water. Add some of the cherry mixture to dissolved cornstarch. Return to
saucepan. Bring to a boil. Stir in sugar.
Adjust sweetness, adding more sugar if
necessary. Cook for 5 minutes until thickened. Cool. Add reserved cherries. Chill.

Serve plain or, if desired, garnish
with sour cream.

Serves 6.

Baby Spinach Salad

- 1 pound baby or regular spinach
  leaves
- 8 red radishes
- 3 shallots or scallions
- 1 small cucumber
- ½ cup pitted black olives
- 1 red onion
- ½ to 1 pint cherry tomatoes
- 1 15-ounce can artichoke hearts
  (optional)
- 1 14-ounce can white asparagus
  (optional)
- 1 hard-boiled egg, chopped
  (for garnish)

Tear spinach into bite-size pieces. Slice
radishes, shallots or scallions, cucumber,
olives, and onion, and add to spinach.
Add cherry tomatoes. Cut artichoke
hearts in half and marinate in Italian
dressing. Before serving, toss lemon
vinaigrette dressing into salad. Serve on
individual plates. Place artichoke halves
and white asparagus on side of salad.
Sprinkle with chopped egg.

Serves 6 to 8.

Baby Spinach Salad.

Lemon Vinaigrette Dressing

- 2 tablespoons lemon juice
- 2 tablespoons white wine vinegar
- 6 tablespoons olive oil
- 1 garlic clove, minced
- ½ teaspoon dried mustard (optional)
- ½ teaspoon seasoned salt
- ½ teaspoon oregano
- Freshly ground pepper

Combine all ingredients and refrigerate until ready to serve.

Variation: Substitute a small heart of romaine lettuce cut into small bite-size pieces for part of spinach leaves.

Broccoli Mushroom Crepes

Crepes are the French answer to blintzes. Since these are rich, they are not for the calorie-conscious, but they are well worth the effort, and are a scrumptious change from cheese blintzes.

Crepes
- 1 cup flour
- 1 cup milk
- 3 eggs
- 2 tablespoons vegetable oil
- ¼ teaspoon salt

Blend all ingredients until smooth. If prepared with a mixer, let mixture rest 30 minutes before proceeding.

To make crepes: put a little oil in a 7-inch frying pan, and heat until hot. Add enough batter to cover bottom of pan thinly (about 3 tablespoons). Tip out excess batter. As soon as batter appears dull, and edges have begun to brown, flip onto other side. Lightly brown. Flip crepe onto waxed paper and repeat with remaining batter. Regrease pan occasionally between crepes. Stack crepes between sheets of waxed paper.

Mornay Sauce

- 5 tablespoons butter
- 4 tablespoons flour
- 2 cups milk
- Salt to taste
- Pepper to taste
- ¼ cup grated Swiss cheese
- ⅛ teaspoon nutmeg
- ½ teaspoon Dijon mustard (optional)
- 6 ounces chopped mushrooms sautéed in 1 to 2 tablespoons of butter with a little lemon juice
- ½ cup half-and-half or milk

Broccoli
- 1 bunch cooked fresh broccoli spears or 2 10-ounce packages of barely cooked frozen broccoli spears
- ¼ cup Parmesan cheese
- Paprika for garnish

Melt 4 tablespoons butter in a saucepan. Remove from heat and add flour. Stir well. Return to moderate heat. Add milk gradually and stir in cheese, nutmeg, and mustard. Add sautéed chopped mushrooms with juice. Reserve half of this sauce for crepe filling. Thin remainder of sauce with half-and-half or milk. This will be poured over the crepes.

To assemble crepes: Put a cooked broccoli spear into each crepe. Add some mornay sauce and roll up like a cigar. Place in a greased shallow casserole dish in a single layer. When all crepes have been used, cover with thinned mornay sauce. Dot with 1 tablespoon melted butter and sprinkle with Parmesan cheese. Garnish with paprika. Broil until lightly browned, about 5 minutes or less. Otherwise, refrigerate and reheat in a 350-degree-F oven for 20 minutes.

Serves 6 to 8.

Note: These crepes also work well with fresh asparagus spears instead of broccoli.

Cheese Blintzes.

Cheese Blintzes

Cheese Blintzes are synonymous with Shavuot. They are easy to make with this fail-proof recipe.

- 2 eggs
- 2 tablespoons vegetable oil
- 1 cup milk or water
- ¾ cup sifted flour
- ½ teaspoon salt
- Margarine or butter for frying

In blender, combine eggs, oil, milk or water, flour, and salt, and blend well. Refrigerate 30 minutes. In a 7-inch hot skillet, melt 1 teaspoon butter and wipe off excess. Pour enough batter into skillet over medium heat to cover and drain off excess. Cook until underside is brown. Remove from pan and place on wax paper. Continue until all batter is used, adding more butter as needed. Stack blintzes between sheets of waxed paper.

Cheese Filling
- 1 pound dry cottage cheese or farmer cheese
- 4 ounces cream cheese, softened
- 2 egg yolks, beaten
- 3 to 4 tablespoons sugar
- ¼ teaspoon vanilla
- ½ teaspoon lemon rind (optional)

Combine ingredients and mix until smooth.

To assemble: Place 1 heaping tablespoon of filling in the center of the browned side of the blintz. Turn in two opposite ends and fold to make an envelope. Fry in large buttered skillet on both sides over medium heat. Serve with sour cream or jam.

Serves 6.

Spinach and Ricotta Manicotti with Tomato Sauce

These tender homemade shells resemble blintzes but the bottoms are not browned. They are much more tender than store-bought manicotti shells.

Shells
- 4 eggs
- 1 cup flour
- ½ teaspoon salt
- 1 cup water
- Oil, butter, or nonstick coating

In blender, combine eggs, flour, water, and salt and blend until smooth. Let stand ½ hour. Heat a 7-inch skillet and brush lightly with oil or butter. Pour 3 tablespoons batter into skillet and cook until top is dry, but do not brown bottom. Turn onto waxed paper. Repeat until all batter is used. Cool and stack between sheets of waxed paper.

Filling
- 1 12-ounce package frozen chopped spinach
- 2 scallions with greens, chopped
- 1 tablespoon vegetable oil
- 1 pound ricotta cheese
- ⅓ cup Parmesan cheese
- 2 eggs, well beaten
- ¼ teaspoon nutmeg
- ½ teaspoon salt
- ¼ teaspoon pepper
- 1 tablespoon fresh parsley, finely chopped

Defrost spinach and drain all liquid. Sauté scallions in oil until limp and golden brown. Mix with spinach. Add ricotta, Parmesan cheese, egg, nutmeg, salt, pepper, and parsley. Mix well. Place ¼ cup filling in center of each shell and roll like a cigar.

Variation: Omit spinach, scallions, and oil. Increase ricotta cheese to 1¼ pounds. Add 1 cup shredded mozzarella cheese.

Tomato Sauce

- 1 medium onion, finely chopped
- 2 cloves garlic, crushed
- 2 tablespoons olive oil
- 1 28-ounce can Italian tomatoes, undrained
- 1 6-ounce can tomato paste
- 1½ cups water
- 2 teaspoons sugar
- 1 teaspoon Italian seasoning (optional)
- 1 teaspoon oregano
- 1 teaspoon basil
- 1 teaspoon thyme
- 1 teaspoon dried sage
- 2 teaspoons salt
- ¼ teaspoon pepper
- 1 slice lemon
- 2 tablespoons dry red wine (optional)

Sauté onion and garlic in oil until limp. Add remaining ingredients except wine. Cover and simmer for 30 to 45 minutes. Add wine and stir.

Preheat oven to 350 degrees F. Place 2 cups sauce on the bottom of a casserole dish. Place one layer of manicotti on sauce. Cover with additional sauce. Sprinkle top with Parmesan cheese. Bake, covered with foil, for 30 minutes.

Makes about 12 manicotti.

Blueberry Streusel Coffee Cake

- ½ cup softened butter or margarine
- 1 cup sugar
- 2 eggs
- 1 teaspoon vanilla or lemon extract
- 2 cups flour
- 2 teaspoons baking powder
- ¼ teaspoon salt
- ½ cup milk
- 1 pint fresh or frozen unsweetened blueberries

Streusel Topping
- ½ cup sugar
- ½ cup flour
- 1 teaspoon cinnamon
- ¼ teaspoon nutmeg
- 4 tablespoons margarine
- ¼ cup chopped almonds or walnuts

Preheat oven to 350 degrees F. Grease and flour a 9-inch springform pan or spray with a nonstick coating. For streusel topping, combine sugar, flour, cinnamon, and nutmeg. Cut in margarine until mixture is crumbly. Add nuts and toss lightly. Set aside.

For cake: Combine butter or margarine with sugar and beat until well blended. Add eggs and beat until fluffy. Add vanilla or lemon extract and mix. Combine dry ingredients and add alternately with milk. Beat until smooth. Spread batter into prepared pan and sprinkle blueberries on top. Cover with streusel topping and bake until toothpick inserted in the center comes out clean, about 50 to 60 minutes. Cool and loosen with a knife from the pan. Cut into squares.

Serves 10.

Blueberry Streusel Coffee Cake.

Rugelach.

Ginger Carrot Soup

The recipe for this lovely soup was given to me by a superb cook and good friend, Judy Wahler of Caldwell, New Jersey.

- 2 tablespoons butter or margarine
- 1½ cups diced onion
- 10 to 12 carrots, peeled and sliced (about 4 cups)
- 1½ tablespoons fresh ginger, grated
- 4 cups vegetable broth
- ¼ cup fresh orange juice
- 2½ cups half-and-half or milk
- Salt to taste
- Paprika to taste
- Sour cream
- Fresh parsley, chopped

Melt butter or margarine in a saucepan. Add onions and cook until transparent, about 10 minutes. Add carrots, ginger, and vegetable broth. Cover and simmer for 25 to 30 minutes or until carrots are tender. Cool. Place in a blender or food processor and puree. Return to saucepan and add orange juice and half-and-half or milk. Season with salt and paprika. Before serving, heat but do not boil. Serve with a dollop of sour cream and a sprinkling of parsley.

Serves 6 to 8.

Note: To make this recipe pareve or less creamy, increase the vegetable broth to 6 cups, use margarine instead of butter, and omit the half-and-half or use just a little nondairy creamer to lighten. Omit sour cream.

Rugelach

These wonderful miniature Danish are made with vanilla ice cream instead of cream cheese. A pareve dough recipe follows.

Dough
- 1 stick butter or margarine, softened
- 1 cup vanilla ice cream
- 2 cups flour
- 1 teaspoon vanilla

Filling
- ½ cup currants
- ½ cup finely chopped walnuts
- ¼ to ⅓ cup sugar
- 1 teaspoon cinnamon
- Strawberry or raspberry all-fruit spread

Combine butter or margarine, ice cream, flour, and vanilla. Beat or knead until well mixed and smooth. Form dough into ball, wrap in plastic wrap, and refrigerate for about an hour.

Preheat oven to 375 degrees F. Spray cookie sheet with nonstick cooking spray or grease lightly. Combine currants, walnuts, sugar, and cinnamon. Divide dough into four equal parts. Shape into balls. On floured board, roll ball into a circle. Brush with a thin coating of fruit spread. Sprinkle with cinnamon/sugar mixture. Cut circle into about 10 pie-shaped wedges. Starting at wide end, roll up toward point, and pinch end to seal. Repeat with remaining dough and sugar mixture. Bake about 20 minutes or until lightly browned.

Pareve dough for rugelach
- ¼ cup warm water
- 1 package dry yeast
- ½ cup pareve margarine
- 2 cups flour
- 1 teaspoon salt
- 2 slightly beaten eggs

Dissolve yeast in warm water and set aside. Cut margarine into flour and salt, and add eggs and yeast mixture. Form dough into a ball, wrap with plastic wrap, and refrigerate for several hours. Proceed as with nonpareve dough recipe, but bake in 350 degree F oven 20 minutes.

Broiled Halibut with Capers

- 6 fresh halibut steaks (³/₄-inch thick—about 4 ounces each)

Marinade
- ½ cup olive oil
- ½ cup vermouth
- 1 tablespoon lemon juice
- ½ teaspoon salt
- 2 teaspoons fresh chopped parsley
- Pinch of thyme
- Pinch of pepper
- 1 teaspoon lemon zest
- 2 tablespoons drained capers
- Fresh parsley sprigs

Combine all marinade ingredients and marinate halibut for 30 to 60 minutes. Broil or grill fish, allowing about 5 to 6 minutes per side or until fish flakes easily when tested with a fork. Garnish with sprigs of fresh parsley. If desired, serve with lemon-wine butter sauce.
Serves 6.

Lemon-Wine Butter Sauce

- 1 tablespoon butter
- 3 tablespoons chopped shallots
- 1 tablespoon capers, drained
- 2 tablespoons fresh lemon juice
- 4 tablespoons white wine
- 1 teaspoon lemon zest

Melt butter in skillet. Add shallots and sauté until limp, about 5 minutes. Add remaining ingredients, heat through, and remove from heat. Pour over halibut or serve in a bowl on the side.

Note: For more sauce, double the recipe.

Herbed Orzo

Orzo is a delightful tiny pasta resembling rice.

- 2 cups orzo
- 3 tablespoons butter
- ⅓ cup toasted pine nuts
- ¼ cup pimiento or chopped roasted red pepper (optional)
- 1 tablespoon fresh lemon juice
- Salt to taste
- Pepper to taste
- 2 tablespoons minced parsley or cilantro
- 2 tablespoons minced mint (optional)

Prepare orzo according to package directions. Drain well. Stir in pieces of butter, pine nuts, pimiento or roasted red pepper, lemon juice, salt, pepper, parsley or cilantro, and mint.
Serves 6.

White/Dark Chocolate Cheesecake

This scrumptious cheesecake is perfect for Shavuot. Its rich, creamy flavor is enhanced by white chocolate. There is a lovely contrast between the white chocolate filling and the darker chocolate crust as well as the chocolate curls for garnishing.

- 1¼ cups plain chocolate cookies
- 4 tablespoons butter, melted
- 2 tablespoons sugar
- ¼ cup chopped walnuts
- 3 8-ounce packages cream cheese
- ¾ cup sugar
- 2 large eggs
- 1 teaspoon vanilla
- 1 teaspoon lemon juice
- ¾ cup sour cream
- 6 ounces white chocolate

Preheat oven to 425 degrees F. In food processor, process chocolate cookies until finely crushed. Add melted butter, 2 tablespoons of sugar, and walnuts; blend. Pat crumb mixture into a greased 9-inch springform pan and bake for 10 minutes. Let cool.

Beat cream cheese and ¾ cup of sugar together. Add eggs, one at a time, and beat mixture well after each addition.

Sautéed Zucchini

- 3 garlic cloves, minced
- 3 tablespoons olive oil
- 8 small zucchini (about 1¾ pounds)
- Juice of 1 large lemon
- Salt to taste
- Pinch of cayenne pepper or red pepper flakes (optional)

Heat oil in wok or frying pan. Add garlic and sauté until soft. Add zucchini and sauté for a few minutes, turning occasionally until zucchini begins to brown. Cover and cook an additional minute or two. Sprinkle with lemon juice and salt. A little sprinkling of cayenne pepper or red pepper flakes will give this dish some zip, but go easy.
Serves 6.

Add vanilla, lemon juice, and sour cream and beat until well blended. Melt white chocolate in top of double boiler over hot but not simmering water. Fold melted white chocolate into the cream cheese batter. Pour this mixture into cooled crust. Bake in a 425-degree-F oven for 10 minutes. Reduce oven temperature to 250 degrees F and bake for 30 minutes or until center is set.

White Chocolate Ganache

- 6 ounces white chocolate
- ¼ cup half-and-half
- 2 tablespoons white chocolate liqueur (Truffles® or white creme de cacao)
- Dark and milk chocolate curls

Melt white chocolate in top of double boiler over hot water, stirring frequently. Add half-and-half. Stir until well blended. Add liqueur. Cool.

When cheesecake has cooled, remove from pan. Pour white chocolate mixture on top and sides. Garnish with dark and milk chocolate curls made by scraping dark and milk chocolate with vegetable peeler onto top of cake.
Serves 10 to 12.

CHAPTER ONE
ROSH HASHANAH

L' SHANAH TOVAH

Liturgy   Traditional

CHAPTER TWO
YOM KIPPUR

KOL NIDREI

Traditional
Arranged by Velvel Pasternak

AVINU MALKEINU

Liturgy   Folk song
Arranged by Velvel Pasternak

Blowing the Shofar for Rosh Hashanah in Jerusalem.

CHAPTER THREE
SUKKOT, SHEMINI ATZERET, AND SIMHAT TORAH

HASUKKAH MAH YAFFAH

Folk song

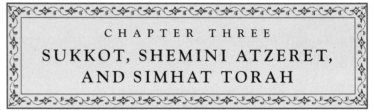

SHLOMIT BONAH SUKKAT SHALOM

Music and lyrics by Naomi Shemer

B'SIMCHAT TORAH

Music by Y. Paikov
Arranged by Velvel Pasternak

MAOZ TZUR

Traditional

Hebrew verse: Mordecai Ben Isaac
English verse: Gustav Gottheil and M. Jastrow

HANUKA, HANUKA

Music and lyrics by Flory Jagoda

C H A P T E R   F O U R
H A N U K K A H

NER LI

Lyrics by L. Kipnis
Music by D. Sambursky
Arranged by Velvel Pasternak

Candles are lit and gifts are exchanged during Hanukkah.

IN SHU, SHU, SHUSHAN

Music courtesy of Education Department
of the United Synagogue of America

A WICKED MAN

Folk song
Arranged by Velvel Pasternak

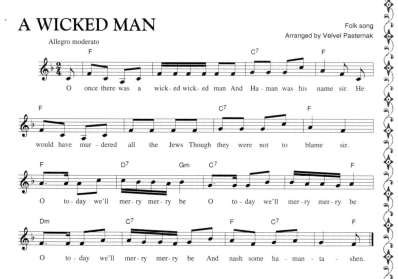

ANI PURIM

Lyrics by L. Kipnis
Music by N. Nardi
Arranged by Velvel Pasternak

MAH NISHTANAH

Israeli
Arranged by Velvel Pasternak

DAYEINU

Hagada

Folk song

L'SHANAH HABA'AH

Folk song
Arranged by Velvel Pasternak

CHAD GADYA

SALEINU

METRIC CONVERSION CHART

WHEN YOU KNOW	MULTIPLY BY	TO FIND
ounces	28	grams
pounds	0.45	kilograms
teaspoons	5	milliliters
tablespoons	15	milliliters
fluid ounces	30	milliliters
cups	0.24	liters
pints	0.47	liters
quarts	0.95	liters
gallons (U.S.)	3.8	liters
gallons (U.K.)	4.5	liters
temperature (Fahrenheit)	$(-32) \times \frac{5}{9}$	temperature (Celsius)

FURTHER READING FOR ADULTS AND CHILDREN

This section is a select and limited guide to sources and resources pertaining to the Jewish holidays. There is a good deal of material available and more coming out each year. Because of the changing nature of the material, please check whether books and stores are still current.

General Holiday Books for Adults

CELEBRATION series (Rosh Hashanah and Yom Kippur, Hanukkah, Purim, and Pesah). New York: Women's League for Conservative Judaism.

Gaster, Theodore. *Festivals of the Jewish Year.* 1952; reprinted New York: William Morrow, 1971.

Goodman, Philip, ed. *JPS Holiday Anthologies* (Rosh Hashanah, Yom Kippur, Sukkot, and Simhat Torah, Purim, Passover, and Shavuot). Philadelphia: Jewish Publication Society.

Greenberg, Rabbi Irving. *The Jewish Way: Living the Holidays.* New York: Touchstone Publishers (Simon and Schuster), 1985.

Renberg, Dalia Hardof. *The Family Guide to Jewish Holidays.* New York: Adama Books, 1985.

Schauss, Hayyim. *The Jewish Festivals: History and Observance.* Cincinnati: 1938; reprinted New York: Schocken Books, 1977.

Strassfeld, Michael. *Jewish Holidays: A Guide and Commentary.* New York: Harper and Row, 1985.

Waskow, Arthur. *Seasons of Our Joy: A Modern Guide to the Jewish Holidays.* Boston: Beacon Press, 1982.

Wolfson, Ron. *The Art of Jewish Living* series (Hanukkah and Pesah). New York: Federation of Jewish Men's Clubs, 1990.

A late nineteenth-century oil painting titled Sukkoth, *by Leopold Pilichowski.*

Jewish Holiday Cookbooks

General

Banin, Israela. *Entertaining on the Jewish Holidays*. New York: SPI Books, 1992.

Feurstadt, Ivy, and Melinda Strauss, eds. *New Kosher Cuisine for All Seasons*. Berkeley, Calif.: Ten Speed Press, 1993.

Greenberg, Elayne. *The Guide to Traditional Jewish Holiday Cooking and Customs*. Santa Monica, Calif.: Write Image Press, 1991 (a revival of Fannie Engle and Gertrude Blair's *The Jewish Festival Cookbook*).

Greene, Gloria Kauffer. *The Jewish Holiday Cookbook: An International Collection of Recipes and Customs*. New York: Times Books (Random House division), 1985.

Nathan, Joan. *The Jewish Holiday Kitchen*, new and revised edition. New York: Schocken Books, 1988.

Zeidler, Judy. *The Gourmet Jewish Cook*. New York: William Morrow, 1988.

Passover Cookbooks

AvRutick, Frances R. *The Complete Passover Cookbook*. New York: Jonathan David, 1981.

Friedland, Susan R. *The Passover Table*. New York: Harper-Perennial, 1994.

Rousso, Nira. *The Passover Gourmet*. New York: Adama Books, 1987.

Children's Holiday Books

There are many fine children's holiday books. The following list is a small selection. These books, if in print, can be purchased, or borrowed from synagogue and Jewish community center libraries.

General Holiday Books

Cashman, Greer Faye. *Jewish Days and Holidays*. New York: SBS Publishing, 1979.

Drucker, Malka, compiler. *Treasury of Jewish Holidays*. Boston: Little Brown, 1994.

Ganz, Yaffa. *Savta, Simcha and the Cinnamon Tree*. Spring Valley, N.Y.: Phillip Feldheim, 1984. (grades 1 to 4)

Greenberg, Melanie Hope. *Celebrations, Our Jewish Holidays*. Philadelphia: Jewish Publication Society. (preschool to grade 3)

Jaffe, Nina. *The Uninvited Guest and Other Jewish Holiday Tales*. New York: Scholastic, 1993.

Labovitz, Annette and Eugene. *Time for My Soul: A Treasury of Jewish Stories for Our Holy Days*. Northvale, N.J.: Jason Aronson, 1987. (grades 6 and above)

Lazar, Wendy Phillips. *The Jewish Holiday Book*. New York: Doubleday, 1977. (grades 3 to 7)

Shevrin, Aliza, trans. *Holiday Tales of Shalom Aleichem*. New York: Scribner, 1979. (grades 5 to 9)

Sofer, Barbara. *Holiday Adventures of Achbar*. Rockville, Md.: Kar-Ben, 1983. (grades 2 to 5)

Taylor, Sidney. *Danny Loves a Holiday*. New York: E. P. Dutton, 1980. (preschool to grade 3)

Weilerstein, Sadie Rose; ill. by Marilyn Hirsh. *The Best of K'tonton*. Phila.: Jewish Publication Society, 1980. (preschool to grade 5)

Zelben, Jane Breskin. *Beni's Little Library: A Jewish Holiday Boxed Set*. New York: Henry Holt, 1993. (preschool)

Rosh Hashanah and Yom Kippur

Drucker, Malka. *Rosh Hashanah and Yom Kippur: Sweet Beginnings*. New York: Holiday House, 1981. (grades 4 to 8)

Greenfield, Howard. *Rosh Hashanah and Yom Kippur*. New York: Henry Holt, 1979. (grades 4 to 8)

Sukkot and Simchat Torah

Chaikin, Miriam. *Shake a Palm Branch: The Story and Meaning of Succoth and Simchat Torah*. New York: Clarion Books, 1984. (grades 4 to 8)

Drucker, Malka. *Sukkot: A Time to Rejoice*. New York: Holiday House, 1982. (grades 4 to 8)

Hanukkah

Adler, David. *A Picture Book of Hanukkah*. New York: Holiday House, 1982. (grades K to 3)

Burns, Marilyn. *The Hanukkah Book*. New York: Four Winds, 1981. (grades 2 to 6)

Chaikin, Miriam. *Light Another Candle: The Story and Meaning of Chanukah*. New York: Clarion Books, 1981. (grades 4 to 8)

Drucker, Malka. *Hanukkah: Eight Nights, Eight Lights*. New York: Holiday House, 1980. (grades 4 to 8)

Greenfield, Howard. *Chanukah*. New York: Henry Holt, 1976. (grades 4 to 8)

Purim

Chaikin, Miriam. *Make Noise, Make Merry: The Story of Purim*. New York: Clarion Books, 1983. (grades 4 to 8)

Greenfield, Howard. *Purim*. New York: Henry Holt, 1982. (grades 5 to 8)

Passover

Adler, David A. *A Picture Book of Passover*. New York: Holiday House, 1982. (grades 1 to 5)

Chaikin, Miriam. *Ask Another Question: The Story and Meaning of Passover*. New York: Clarion Books, 1985. (grades 4 to 8)

Drucker, Malka. *Passover: A Season of Delight*. New York: Holiday House, 1981. (grades 4 to 8)

Goldin, Barbara Diamond. *A Passover Journey: A Seder Companion*. New York: Viking, 1994 (grades 3 to 6)

Greenfield, Howard. *Passover*. New York: Henry Holt, 1978. (grades 4 to 8)

Marcus, Audrey, and Raymond Zwerin. *But This Night Is Different: A Passover Experience*. New York: Union of American Hebrew Congregations, 1980. (preschool to grade 2)

Rosen, Anne, Jonathan, and Norman. *A Family Passover*. Philadelphia: Jewish Publication Society, 1980. (grades K to 5)

Sherman, Ori. *The Four Questions*. New York: Dial Books, 1989. (grades K to 5)

RESOURCES

Stores that sell Jewish books often sell Judaica as well. Some shops sell exclusively one or the other. The following list includes all categories.

USA

Arizona
Israel Connection
5539 N. 7th St.
Phoenix, AZ 85014

California
Afikomen
3042 Claremont Ave.
Berkeley, CA 94705

Atara's Hebrew Book and Gift
   Store
450 N. Fairfax Ave.
Los Angeles, CA 90036

Ben Yehuda Street
4382 Katella Ave.
Los Alamitos, CA 90720

Bob & Bob Fine Jewish Gifts
151 Forest Ave.
Palo Alto, CA 94301

Golden Dreidle
1835 Newport Blvd.,
   Suite A-113
Costa Mesa, CA 92627

House of David
12826 Victoria Blvd.
North Hollywood, CA 91606

Jerusalem Fair
14245 Ventura Blvd.
Sherman Oaks, CA 91423

Jerusalem West
6512 El Cajun Blvd.
San Diego, CA 92115

Mitzvah Store 613
9400 W. Pico Blvd.
Los Angeles, CA 90035

Treasures of Judaica
University of Judaism
15600 Mulholland Dr.
Los Angeles, CA 90077

Colorado
Boutique Judaica
5078 E. Hampden Ave.
Denver, CO 80222

Connecticut
Jewish Book and Gift Shoppe
360 Amity Rd.
Woodbridge, CT 06525

Jewish Book Shop
570 Whalley Ave.
New Haven, CT 06511

The Judaica Book Shop
262 South Whitney St.
New Haven, CT 06105

Ya-El Imports Inc.
5 Old Town Park Rd. #88
New Milford, CT 06776

Florida
American Israeli Religious
   Bookstore
1357 Washington Ave.
Miami, FL 33139

Chosen Gift Shop
7146 S. W. 117th Ave.
Miami, FL 33183

Holyland Judaica
5650 Stirling Rd., Suite 19
Hollywood, FL 33021

Judaica Enterprise
1125 N. E. 163rd St.
North Miami Beach, FL 33162

Ner-Tamid
104 Lake Paula Dr.
West Palm Beach, FL 33411

Torah Treasures
4016 Chase Ave.
Miami Beach, FL 33140

Georgia
Chosen Treasures
5920 Roswell Rd.
Atlanta, GA 30328

Judaica Corner
2183 Briarcliff Rd.
Atlanta, GA 30329

Illinois
Richard Bitterman
1701 Chase Ave.
Chicago, IL 60626

Chicago Hebrew Book Store
2942 West Devon Ave.
Chicago, IL 60645

An illuminated Haggadah open to the end of the section discussing the four types of children.

Feldman Gallery
1815 St. Johns Ave.
Highland Park, IL 60035

Hamakor Gallery, Ltd.
4150 W. Dempster
Skokie, IL 60076

Rosenblum's Hebrew Books
2906 West Devon Ave.
Chicago, IL 60659

Maryland
Central Hebrew Bookstore
228 Reistertown Rd.
Baltimore, MD 21208

Israeli Accents
4838 Boiling Brook Pkwy.
Rockville, MD 20852

Jewish Book Store of Greater
    Washington
11250 Georgia Ave.
Wheaton, MD 20902

Jewish Heritage Center
    Book Shoppe
15 Lloyd St.
Baltimore, MD 21202

Pern's Hebrew Book
    and Gift Store
7012 Reistertown Road
Baltimore, MD 21215

Massachussetts
Brandeis Bookstore
415 South St.
Waltham, MA 02154

Gesher Jewish Books
88 Grantwood Dr.
Amherst, MA 01002

Israel Bookshop
410 Harvard St.
Brookline, MA 02146

Kolbo Fine Jewish Gifts
435 Harvard St.
Brookline, MA 02146

Sabbath Lights
419 Worcester Rd.
Framingham, MA 01701

Michigan
Borenstein Bookstore
25242 Greenfield Rd.
Oak Park, MI 48237

Esther's Judaica
4301 Orchard Lake #231
W. Bloomfield, MI 48323

Spitzer's Hebrew Books
21770 West Eleven Mile Rd.
Southfield, MI 48076

Tradition Tradition
17235 Shervilla Pl.
Southfield, MI 48075

Minnesota
Brochins Book and Gift Shop
4813 Minnetonka Blvd.
Minneapolis, MN 55416

Elijah's Cup
8112 Minnetonka Blvd.
St. Louis Park, MN 55416

Missouri
The Source
11044 Olive St.
St. Louis, MS 63141

New Jersey
Behrman House
235 Watchung Ave.
West Orange, NJ 07052

CBL Fine Art
459 Pleasant Valley Way
West Orange, NJ 07052

Judaica House
19 Grand Ave.
Englewood, NJ 07631

Kesser Gifts and Judaica
216 Main Ave.
Passaic, NJ 07055

Precious Heirlooms
67 Childs Rd.
Bernardsville, NJ 07924

Priceless Possessions
176 Rt. 17N
Paramus, NJ 07652

Sky Book Store
1923 Springfield Ave.
Maplewood, NJ 07040

Trio Gifts
246 Raritan Ave.
Highland Park, NJ 08904

New York
Ben Ari Arts Ltd.
11 Ave. A
New York, NY 10009

Eichler's Book Store
5004 13th Ave.
Brooklyn, NY 11219

Feller's Judaica and Gift Gallery
1205 Lexington Ave.
New York, NY 10028

An ornate Hanukkah lamp from Vienna by Josef Kohn. The hanukiyah *is made from hammered silver, embossed and then cast.*

The Jewish Quarter
150 Mamaroneck Ave.
White Plains, NY 10601

J. Levine Religious Supplies Inc.
5 W. 30th St.
New York, NY 10001

Judaica of Great Neck
107 Middle Neck Rd.
Great Neck, NY 11021

Judaica Plus
530 Central Ave.
Cedarhurst, NY 11516

Judaica Unlimited
400 Hempstead Tpk.
W. Hempstead, NY 11512

Kitov Book Store
1847 Mott Ave.
Far Rockaway, NY 11691

Presentations—Contemporary
    Judaica & Synagogue Art
200 Lexington Ave., Suite 506
New York, NY 10016

Riverdale Judaica
3706 Riverdale Ave.
Riverdale, NY 10463

Shoshana
49 South St.
New City, NY 10956

Stavsky Hebrew Book Store
147 Essex St.
New York, NY 10002

Tradition
932 S. Winton Rd.
Rochester, NY 14618

West Side Judaica
2412 Broadway
New York, NY 10024

Yussel's Place
59 Merrick Ave.
Merrick, NY 11566

North Carolina
Mazal Tov Gifts
6325-125 Falls of Neuse St.
Raleigh, NC 27615

Ohio

Frank's Hebrew Bookstore
1647 Lee Rd.
Cleveland, OH 44118

Hebrew Union College
3101 Clifton Ave.
Cincinnati, OH 45220

Jacob's Judaica Book
    and Gift Center
13896 Cedar Rd.
University Heights, OH 44118

Pennsylvania

Bala Judaica
22 Bala Ave.
Bala Cynwyd, PA 19004

Designs by Brenda
1110 Grouse Dr.
Pittsburgh, PA 15243

Graetz College
Melrose Ave.
Melrose Park, PA 19004

Neo Judaica
733 Walnut St.
Philadelphia, PA 19106

Pinsker's Judaica Center
2028 Murray Ave.
Pittsburgh, PA 15217

Rosenberg's Hebrew Book Store
6408 Castor Ave.
Philadelphia, PA 19149

Rosen's Hebrew Book Store
6743 Castor Ave.
Philadelphia, PA 19149

Rhode Island

Tikvah Traditions
727 Hope St.
Providence, RI 02906

Texas

Elijah's Cup
5711 Dumfries
Houston, TX 77096

Jumbo Judaica of Texas
7726 Claridge
Houston, TX 77071

Tradition
7817 Candle Ln.
Houston, TX 77071

Canada

Ontario

Aleph Bet Judaica
3453 Bathurst St.
Toronto, Ont. M6A 2C3

Israel's the Judaica Center
897 Eglinton West
Toronto, Ont. M6C 2C1

Matana Judaica
494 Steeles Ave. West
Thornhill, Ont. L4J 6X3

Miriam's Gift Gallery
3007 Bathurst St.
Toronto, Ont. M6B 383

Negev Book and Gift Store
3509 Bathurst St.
Toronto, Ont. M6A 2C5

Quebec

Bibliophile
5519 Queen Mary Rd.
Montreal, Que. H3X 1V4

Kotel Jewish Book and Gift Shop
6414 Victoria Ave.
Montreal, Que. H3W 2S6

Rodal's Jewish Book
    and Gift Shop
4689 Van Horne Ave.
Montreal, Que. H3W 1H8

Museum Gift Shops

The Baris Shop
Spertus College of Judaica
618 S. Michigan Ave.
Chicago, IL 60605

B'nai B'rith Klutznick Museum
1640 Rhode Island Ave. NW
Washington, DC 20036

The Cooper Store
    (The Jewish Museum)
1109 Fifth Ave.
New York, NY 10028

The Jewish Museum San
    Francisco Museum Shop
121 Steuart St.
San Francisco, CA 94105

National Museum of
    American Jewish History
    Museum Shoppe
55 N. Fifth St.
Philadelphia, PA

Other Sources

Synagogue sisterhood gift shops, Jewish community center shops, conventions, and book fairs all are excellent sources for the acquisition of Jewish books and Judaica.

1-800-JUDAISM
    (catalog available)
2028 Murray Ave.
Pittsburgh, PA 15217

Galerie Robin Ltd.
    (catalog available)
P. O. Box 42275
Cincinnati, OH 45242-0275
800-635-8279

Hamakor Judaica, Inc.
    (catalog available)
The Source for Everything Jewish
P. O. Box 48836
Niles, IL 60714-0836
800-426-2567

Jewish Book Council
    (book lists, book fairs,
    National Jewish Book awards)
15 E. 26th St.
New York, NY 10010
212-532-4949

Jewish Publication Society
    (catalog available)
1930 Chestnut St.
Philadelphia, PA 19103
215-564-5925 or 800-355-1165

Jonathan David Company Inc.
    (catalog available)
68-22 Eliot Ave.
Middle Village, NY 11379
718-456-8611

Kar-Ben Copies Inc.
    (catalog available)
6800 Tildenswood Ln.
Rockville, MD 20852
800-4-KARBEN

The Learning Plant
P. O. Box 17233
W. Palm Beach, FL 33416-7233
407-686-9456

Union of American Hebrew
    Congregations Press
    (catalog available)
838 Fifth Ave.
New York, NY 11021
212-249-0100

United Synagogue Book Service
    (catalog available)
155 Fifth Ave.
New York, NY 10010
212-533-7800, Ext. 2003

For Individual Artists

The American Guild of Judaic Art, a not-for-profit organization, consists of nearly four hundred artists and craftspeople from the United States, Israel, and Canada. For further information, write the American Guild of Judaic Art, Box 1794 Murray Hill Station, New York, NY 10156–0609.

Jewish Audio-Visual Sources

Davka Corporation (catalog for
    Judaic software, CD-ROMs,
    and games available)
7074 N. Western
Chicago, IL 60645
312-465-4070
800-621-8227

Ergo Media Inc.
    (video catalog available)
P. O. Box 2037
Teaneck, NJ 07666
201-836-4233
800-695-3746

Media Center
    (video rentals, some sales)
Board of Jewish Education of
    Greater New York
426 W. 58th St.
New York, NY 10019
212-245-8200, Ext. 316

SISU Entertainment Inc./
    Kol Ami (catalog available)
18 W. 27th St. 10th floor
New York, NY 10001
212-779-7944

TARA Publications (music catalog for CDs, cassettes, books, and sheet music)
29 Derby Ave.
Cedarhurst, NY
516-295-2290

TARA-WEST Publications (music fairs, music catalog for CDs, cassettes, books, and sheet music)
28313 Redondo Way South #101
Redondo, WA 98003
206-946-9169

INDEX